N. E. S. C. O. T.   LIBRARY

MARTIN HEIDEGGER

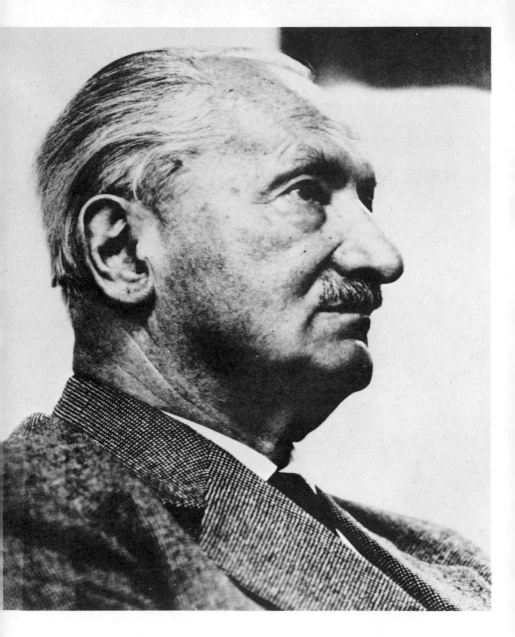

MARTIN HEIDEGGER

An Illustrated Study by

Walter Biemel

Translated by J. L. Mehta

Routledge & Kegan Paul

London and Henley

193 BIE

First published in Great Britain in 1977
by Routledge & Kegan Paul Ltd
39 Store Street,
London WC1E 7DD and
Broadway House,
Newtown Road,
Henley-on-Thames,
Oxon RG9 1EN

Printed in Great Britain by
Lowe & Brydone Printers Ltd
Thetford, Norfolk

ISBN 0 7100 8638 5

30664

FOR MARLY

Contents

Translator's Note

Translating Heidegger or an exposition that stays close to Heidegger's own words, like this one, poses problems which have often been noticed, though not as yet investigated in depth. An added complication arises from the fact that much of Heidegger's thinking, apart from its explicit and implicit concern with the phenomenon of translation in the broadest sense, is itself a mode of translating, a motion within language, a pressuring of language and an experiencing of its pressure. The translator himself is drawn into the very movement of the thought he is seeking to render from one language into another, and is committed to adopting a "philosophy" of translation that is in tune with the concept of translating implicit, though constantly changing, in Heidegger's work. Far from functioning as a neutral agent, the translator has to be something of an advocate seeking to involve the reader in this movement and in the movement taking place in the act of translating, not making it smooth for the reader but rather making him experience the difficulties, the jolts and the strangeness of what is going on here. This is what reading Heidegger is, or should be, in any language.

Where translations of the writings quoted in this book are available, they have been used and referred to. The reader may find it instructive, however, to go back to the original German. Such a movement in search of meaning, too, is part of the *Sache* that is Heidegger's. The difficulty inherent in this whole "matter," of which a translation is itself a part, cannot be lightened by trying to develop a glossary of technical terms used by Heidegger, for there are none.

J. L. Mehta

Introduction

Before we begin with the exposition, a word of explanation may be allowed regarding what is sought here. In a monograph one usually expects an account of unusual events in the life of the author. With this is connected the expectation that these events will furnish a key to the understanding of the creative achievement of that person. It is a widespread view that through the life of a person we can gain access to, even explain, his work—be he a poet, a composer, a painter, a sculptor or a philosopher.

This is not to deny that in certain cases a knowledge of biographical facts can provide considerable insight into the genesis of these productions, though never an explanation. (This term might safely be left to refer to the activity of grasping natural processes, as Wilhelm Dilthey did when he distinguished explaining and understanding.) In the case of Martin Heidegger, however, we are disappointed in this respect. It is not his life from which we can learn something about his work; his work is his life. Gaining access to his life means, therefore, following his creative activity, trying to grasp the leading idea behind this activity, understanding what it is that this activity opens up, how it unfolds, how it is in constant flux. That which his questioning is about must be of concern to us; far from appearing to be just one among many subjects about which questions might be asked, it should exhibit itself as that on which all our questioning and seeking are ultimately grounded, even though we may not be aware of it.

Instead of the capricious occurrences we so often come across in the lives of most people, we find in Heidegger a unique and resolute consistency of creative work, in the service of which is placed everything that ordinarily constitutes material for biographical reporting. This begins to happen quite early in his life, with the present of Franz Brentano's *Von der mannigfachen Bedeutung des Seienden nach Aristoteles* (*On the Manifold Meaning of Being According to Aristotle*), which the student received from Conrad Gröber, later to be Bishop, and which was to become the shock, as it were, and the impetus that drove him on to his own quest. It was a process that continued with the stimulus he received from the "Ontology" (see pp. 9–10) of Carl Braig, a professor of dogmatics, and the attempt to come to grips with Edmund Husserl's *Logische Untersuchungen* (*Logical Investigations*), with his habilitation thesis, *Die Kategorien- und Bedeutungslehre des Duns Scotus* (The Doctrine of Categories and of Judgment in Duns Scotus), written in 1916, the Aristotle interpretations of the early twenties, down to *Sein und Zeit* (*Being and Time*), published in 1927, and *Zur Sache des Denkens* (*On Time and Being*), published in 1969. The building of the cottage in Todtnauberg in 1922 was also in the service of this creative work. For it was in the stillness of the Black Forest that he worked with utmost concentration, and it was here that the lectures and lessons were prepared and the works written, the impact of which is felt throughout the world.

Except for the period in Marburg from 1923 to 1928, Martin Heidegger lived and worked in Freiburg or Todtnauberg. The few journeys that he undertook were also in the service of his creative work and were primarily lecture trips. The political error of 1933 was of short duration, for he resigned his office as the elected Rector soon after in 1934. Hannah Arendt compares this error, not unjustly, with Plato's error. It is superficial to pounce on it in order to discredit Heidegger. Had the error been a result of his philosophical thought, this thinking itself would have come to an end with the correction of the error. What actually happened was just the opposite, for it was after 1934 that his thinking really began to unfold. His long years of university teaching were devoted solely to the task of communicating his experience of thinking.

Our curiosity thus meets with disappointment, as in the case of Immanuel Kant's life, with its outward monotony and uniformity. Is there, then, anything that remains to be said? An attempt must be made to lay bare the exciting experience of thinking behind the apparent monotony of this life.

This cannot, of course, be done simply by picking out some of the results of Heidegger's passionate wrestling and reducing his creative achievement to them. Hegel's dictum that, without the paths that led to them, the results in themselves are lifeless, is pre-eminently true of Heidegger. Near the beginning of the lecture "The Principle of Identity" he says, "When thinking attempts to pursue something that has claimed its attention, it may happen that on the way it undergoes a change. It is advisable, therefore, in what follows to pay attention to the path of thought rather than to its content" (*Identity and Difference*, p. 23). We shall try to follow some of the thought paths opened up by Heidegger. While doing so, we must keep in mind two things. First, these paths were not already in existence and simply trodden by Heidegger. Coming after him, we find it difficult to imagine that these ways did not exist, because it was through them that we came to know Heidegger; the philosophical landscape has changed completely because of Heidegger. Second, the paths sketched here, as on a chart, are only suggestive examples of what sustains them all. Heidegger's thought cannot be circumscribed by them; on the contrary, these paths are only fragments of a unitary thinking that, in all its intensity of concentration, unfolds itself into a network of inquiry not fully understood even today, despite the vastly increasing literature on Heidegger.

The reader must clearly understand that only fragments can be conveyed here. This exposition will have fulfilled its task if it enables the reader to see that Heidegger's creative achievement is not reducible to these examples, and to regard these only as examples of a work that is itself without precedent and parallel. One of the difficulties with such an exposition is that it must confine itself to the examples and is at the same time meant to lead the reader out of this confinement. We shall attempt to accomplish this by showing how these examples lead us on to the central idea in which they all have their origin, or to put it differently, by showing how this central idea always recurs as a leading motif, though not in the sense of bare repetition but rather as a recapitulation which is transformed each time it is taken up anew and which remains always in flux. Heidegger's thinking never comes to a rest, although it always revolves round the same thing. Every time we think we have finally reached the destination and can firmly grasp it, we are thrown into a new questioning that leaves no foothold unshaken and which turns what seemed to be the goal and conclusion into the starting-point for a new questioning. If René Descartes was in search of an unshakable foundation for philosophizing, Heidegger was concerned with putting just this into question. This is not simply an incidental difference between them but is at the root of the distinction Heidegger makes between philosophizing and thinking, as it is clearly formulated at the end of his path of thinking (see Chapter 10). The temptation to make this procedure intelligible with the help of Hegel's dialectic must be avoided. With Hegel, the course of the dialectic is consummated in the return of the Absolute to itself. For Heidegger, there is no such consummation and perfection. His concept of historicity cannot be understood in the Hegelian sense of a return from self-estrangement.

The following exposition is not an interpretation and explanation of Heidegger's thought, but only an attempt to lead the reader to it. Only when each reader comes to grips with this thought-work can he judge for himself whether this attempt to guide him was a help rather than a hindrance.

MARTIN HEIDEGGER

Heidegger's Influence

Regarding Heidegger's influence, we may adduce here the testimony of a contemporary voice. It is a voice that carries weight, that of Hannah Arendt. We quote some passages from her article.[1]*

"Heidegger's 'fame' predates by about eight years the publication of *Sein und Zeit* (*Being and Time*) in 1927; indeed it is open to question whether the unusual success of this book—not just the immediate impact it had inside and outside the academic world but also its extraordinarily lasting influence, with which few of the century's publications can compare—would have been possible if it had not been preceded by the teacher's reputation among the students, in whose opinion, at any rate, the book's success merely confirmed what they had known for many years.

"There was something strange about this early fame, stranger perhaps than the fame of Kafka in the early twenties or of Braque and Picasso in the preceding decade, who were also unknown to what is commonly understood as the public and nevertheless exerted an extraordinary influence. For in Heidegger's case there was nothing tangible on which his fame could have been based, nothing written, save for notes taken at his lectures which circulated among students everywhere. These lectures dealt with texts that were generally familiar; they contained no doctrine that could have been learned, reproduced, and handed on. There was hardly more than a name, but the name traveled all over Germany like the rumor of the hidden king.

"This was something completely different from a 'circle'

* Numbered notes are to be found at the end of the text on pp. 179–80.

centered around and directed by a 'master' (say, the Stefan George circle), which, while well known to the public, still remained apart from it by an aura of secrecy, the *arcana imperii* to which presumably only the circle's members are privy. Here there was neither a secret nor membership; those who heard the rumor were acquainted with one another, to be sure, since they were all students, and there were occasional friendships among them. Later some cliques formed here and there; but there never was a circle and there was nothing esoteric about his following.

"To whom did the rumor spread, and what did it say? In the German universities at the time, after the First World War, there was no rebellion but widespread discontent with the academic enterprise of teaching and learning in those faculties that were more than professional schools, a disquiet that prevailed among students for whom study meant more than preparing for making a living. Philosophy was no breadwinner's study, but rather the study of resolute starvelings who were, for that very reason, all the harder to please. They were in no way disposed toward a wisdom of life or of the world, and for anyone concerned with the solution of all riddles there was available a rich selection of world views and their partisans; it wasn't necessary to study philosophy in order to choose among them.

"But what they wanted they didn't know. The university commonly offered them either the schools—the neo-Kantians, the neo-Hegelians, the neo-Platonists, etc.—or the old academic discipline, in which philosophy, neatly divided into its special fields— epistemology, aesthetics, ethics, logic, and the like—was not so much communicated as drowned in an ocean of boredom. There were, even before Heidegger's appearance, a few rebels against this comfortable and, in its way, quite solid enterprise. Chronologically, there was Husserl and his cry 'To the things themselves': and that meant, 'Away from theories, away from books' toward the establishment of philosophy as a rigorous science which would take its place alongside other academic disciplines.

"This was still a naïve and unrebellious cry, but it was something to which first Scheler and somewhat later Heidegger could appeal. In addition, there was Karl Jaspers in Heidelberg, consciously rebellious and coming from a tradition other than the philosophical. He, as is known, was for a long time on friendly terms with Heidegger, precisely because the rebellious element in Heidegger's enterprise appealed to him as something original and fundamentally philosophical in the midst of the academic talk *about* philosophy.

"What these few had in common was—to put it in Heidegger's words—that they could distinguish 'between an object of scholarship and a matter of thought' (*Aus der Erfahrung des Denkens*, 1947; ["The Thinker as Poet," in *Poetry, Language, Thought*, 1971]) and that they were pretty indifferent to the object of scholarship. At that time the rumor of Heidegger's teaching reached those who knew more or less explicitly about the breakdown of tradition and the 'dark times' (Brecht) which had set in, who therefore held erudition in matters of philosophy to be idle play and who, therefore, were prepared to comply with the academic discipline only because they were concerned with the 'matter of thought' or, as Heidegger would say today, 'thinking's matter' (*Zur Sache des Denkens*, 1969; [*On Time and Being*, 1972]).

"The rumor that attracted them to Freiburg and to the *Privatdozent* who taught there, as somewhat later they were attracted to the young professor at Marburg, had it that there was someone who was actually attaining "the things" that Husserl had proclaimed, someone who knew that these things were not academic matters but the concerns of thinking men—concerns not just of yesterday and today, but from time immemorial—and who, precisely because he knew that the tradition was broken, was discovering the past anew.

"It was technically decisive that, for instance, Plato was not talked *about* and his theory of ideas expounded; rather for an entire semester a single dialogue was pursued and subjected to question step by step, until the time-honored doctrine had disappeared to make room for a set of problems of immediate and urgent relevance. Today this sounds quite familiar, because nowadays so many proceed in this way; but no one did so before Heidegger.

"The rumor about Heidegger put it quite simply: Thinking has come to life again; the cultural treasures of the past, believed to be dead, are being made to speak, in the course of which it turns out that they propose things altogether different from the familiar, worn-out trivialities they had been presumed to say. There exists a teacher; one can perhaps learn to think.

"The hidden king reigned therefore in the realm of thinking, which, although it is completely of this world, is so concealed in it that one can never be quite sure whether it exists at all; and still its inhabitants must be more numerous than is commonly believed. For how, otherwise, could the unprecedented, often underground, influence of Heidegger's thinking and thoughtful reading be explained, extending as it does beyond the circle of students and disciples and beyond what is commonly understood by philosophy? . . .

". . . People followed the rumor about Heidegger in order to learn thinking. What was experienced was that thinking as pure activity—and this means impelled neither by the thirst for knowledge nor by the drive for cognition—can become a passion which not so much rules and oppresses all other capacities and gifts, as it orders them and prevails through them. We are so accustomed to the old opposition of reason versus passion, spirit versus life, that the idea of a *passionate* thinking, in which thinking and aliveness become one, takes us somewhat aback. Heidegger himself once expressed this unification—on the strength of a proven anecdote— in a single sentence, when at the beginning of a course on Aristotle he said, in place of the usual biographical introduction, 'Aristotle was born, worked, and died.'

"That something like Heidegger's passionate thinking exists is indeed, as we can recognize afterward, a condition of the possibility of there being any philosophy at all. But it is more than questionable, especially in our century, that we would ever have discovered this without the existence of Heidegger's thinking. This passionate thinking, which rises out of the simple fact of being-born-in-the-world and now 'thinks recallingly and responsively the meaning that reigns in everything that is' (*Gelassenheit*, 1959, p. 15; [*Discourse on Thinking*, 1966, p. 46]), can no more have a final goal—cognition or knowledge—than can life itself. The end of life is death, but man does not live for death's sake, but because he is a living being; and he does not think for the sake of any result whatever, but because he is a 'thinking, that is, a musing being' [*Gelassenheit*, p. 15; *Discourse on Thinking*, p. 47].

"A consequence of this is that thinking acts in a peculiarly destructive or critical way toward its own results. To be sure, since the philosophical schools of antiquity, philosophers have exhibited an annoying inclination toward system-building, and we often have trouble disassembling the constructions they have built, when trying to uncover what they really thought. This inclination does not stem from thinking itself, but from quite other needs, themselves thoroughly legitimate. If one wished to measure thinking, in its immediate, passionate liveliness, by its results, then one would fare as with Penelope's veil—what was spun during the day would inexorably undo itself again at night, so that the next day it could be begun anew. Each of Heidegger's writings, despite occasional references to what was already published, reads as though he were starting from the beginning and only from time to time taking over the language already coined by him—a language, however, in which the concepts are merely 'trail marks' by which a new course of thought orients itself."

Those who know Martin Heidegger only through his published writings can hardly form an idea of the unique style of his teaching. Even with beginners, he was able in no time to coax them into thinking, not just learning various views or reproducing what they had read, but entering into the movement of thinking. It seemed as if by some miracle the Socratic practice of address and rejoinder had come to life again.

We know that Husserl was so completely possessed by his own ideas that in reality he was engaged in a continuous monologue. There is an anecdote to the effect that after a seminar meeting for advanced students, Husserl said to Heidegger that it had turned out to be an exceptionally successful session. To the question, "In what respect?" Husserl replied, "In regard to the active participation of the students." Actually, only Husserl had talked during the entire period. In Heidegger's seminars there was no such indulging in monologues; indeed, we were specifically warned against it. When we were dealing with a text on which Heidegger's comments were available in his published writings, citing these interpretations was never permitted. Heidegger wanted to listen not to what he had said about it, but to what we were capable of eliciting from the text. These seminars were therefore never lectures under a different name, but they involved working directly with a text. It sometimes happened that, in one semester, we read and tried to understand only two or three pages of a philosopher. But through these pages, which Heidegger had selected carefully, he was so able in leading us to the very core of the thinking of the philosopher we happened to be studying that we achieved greater understanding of it than some gain through years of study. And this, not only of the individual philosopher but also of the historical stream in the midst of which he stood. Without such historical insight, without this historical dimension, no understanding is possible. This was something we experienced quite directly in these seminars, seminars which were so exciting that we left the small seminar room on the first floor of the Freiburg University building as though electrified. The preparation for the next class kept us engaged actually the entire week, and all other seminars and lectures automatically receded into the background. And when a student was asked to prepare a report on the seminar meeting, which was subsequently recorded in the little black progress-report book, our excitement was still more heightened as we waited eagerly for the next session, which Heidegger started off by reading the report and offering his own critique of it.

The keen interest with which Heidegger followed for decades the career of each participant in his seminars was truly amazing, as was the fact that he never failed to remember any one when, years later, his name was mentioned in conversation.

Heidegger was very painstaking in his preparation for these seminar meetings. He left nothing to the inspiration of the moment, to flashes of sudden insight, but worked out carefully the course of thought to be followed during each seminar. Thus we find in his manuscripts explicit plans and notes for these seminars. Although he was thoroughly versed in the texts to be studied, this preparation was carried out by him each time, as was the selection of the particular portion of the text, so that it always led to the heart of the problem posed for discussion.

The Development
of Heidegger's Thought

Heidegger himself has discussed his university education and his development in "My Way to Phenomenology" ("Mein Weg in die Phänomenologie"). Originally written as a contribution to the presentation volume (1963) for Hermann Niemeyer, the essay was published in *On Time and Being* (*Zur Sache des Denkens*).

"My academic studies began in the winter of 1909–10 in theology at the University of Freiburg. But the chief work for the study in theology still left enough time for philosophy which belonged to the curriculum anyhow. Thus both volumes of Husserl's *Logical Investigations* lay on my desk in the theological seminary ever since my first semester there. These volumes belonged to the university library. The date due could be easily renewed again and again. The work was obviously of little interest to the students. But how did it get into this environment so foreign to it?

"I had learned from many references in philosophical periodicals that Husserl's thought was determined by Franz Brentano. Ever since 1907, Brentano's dissertation 'On the Manifold Meaning of Being According to Aristotle' (1862) had been the chief help and guide of my first awkward attempts to penetrate into philosophy. The following question concerned me in a quite vague manner: If being is predicated in manifold meanings, then what is its leading fundamental meaning? What does Being mean? In the last year of my stay at the *Gymnasium*, I stumbled upon the book of Carl Braig, then professor for dogmatics at Freiburg University: 'On

Being. Outline of Ontology.' It had been published in 1896 at the time when he was an associate professor at Freiburg's theological faculty. The larger sections of the work give extensive text passages from Aristotle, Thomas Aquinas and Suarez, always at the end, and in addition the etymology for fundamental ontological concepts.

"From Husserl's *Logical Investigations,* I expected a decisive aid in the questions stimulated by Brentano's dissertation. Yet my efforts were in vain because I was not searching in the right way. I realized this only very much later. Still, I remained so fascinated by Husserl's work that I read in it again and again in the years to follow without gaining sufficient insight into what fascinated me. The spell emanating from the work extended to the outer appearance of the sentence structure and the title page. . . .

"After four semesters I gave up my theological studies and dedicated myself entirely to philosophy. I still attended theological lectures in the years following 1911, Carl Braig's lecture course on dogmatics. My interest in speculative theology led me to do this, above all the penetrating kind of thinking which this teacher concretely demonstrated in every lecture hour. On a few walks when I was allowed to accompany him, I first heard of Schelling's and Hegel's significance for speculative theology as distinguished from the dogmatic system of Scholasticism. Thus the tension between ontology and speculative theology as the structure of metaphysics entered the field of my search.

"Yet at times this realm faded to the background compared with that which Heinrich Rickert treated in his seminars: the two writings of his pupil Emil Lask who was killed as a simple soldier on the Galician front in 1915. Rickert dedicated the third fully revised edition of his work *The Object of Knowledge, Introduction to Transcendental Philosophy,* which was published the same year, 'to my dear friend.' The dedication was supposed to testify to the teacher's benefit derived from this pupil. Both of Emil Lask's writings—*The Logic of Philosophy and the Doctrine of Categories, A Study of the Dominant Realm of Logical Form* (1911) and *The Doctrine of Judgment* (1912)—themselves showed clearly enough the influence of Husserl's *Logical Investigations.*

"These circumstances forced me to delve into Husserl's work

anew. However, my repeated beginning also remained unsatisfactory, because I couldn't get over a main difficulty. It concerned the simple question how thinking's manner of procedure which called itself 'phenomenology' was to be carried out. What worried me about this question came from the ambiguity which Husserl's work showed at first glance.

"The first volume of the work, published in 1900, brings the refutation of psychologism in logic by showing that the doctrine of thought and knowledge cannot be based on psychology. In contrast, the second volume, which was published the following year and was three times as long, contains the description of the acts of consciousness essential for the constitution of knowledge. So it is a psychology after all. What else is section 9 of the fifth investigation concerning 'The Meaning of Brentano's Delimitation of "psychical phenomena" '? Accordingly, Husserl falls back with his phenomenological description of the phenomena of consciousness into the position of psychologism which he had just refuted. But if such a gross error cannot be attributed to Husserl's work, then what is the phenomenological description of the acts of consciousness? Wherein does what is peculiar to phenomenology consist if it is neither logic nor psychology? Does a quite new discipline of philosophy appear here, even one with its own rank and precedence?

"I could not disentangle these questions. I remained without knowing what to do or where to go. I could hardly even formulate the questions with the clarity in which they are expressed here.

"The year 1913 brought an answer. The *Yearbook for Philosophy and Phenomenological Investigation* which Husserl edited began to be published by the publisher Max Niemeyer. The first volume begins with that treatise of Husserl's, of which the very title proclaims the distinctive character and range of phenomenology: 'Ideas Concerning a Pure Phenomenology and Phenomenological Philosophy.'

" 'Pure phenomenology' is the 'fundamental science' of philosophy which is characterized by that phenomenology. 'Pure' means: 'transcendental phenomenology.' However, the 'subjectivity' of the knowing, acting and valuing subject is posited as 'transcendental.' Both terms, 'subjectivity' and 'transcendental,' show that 'phenomenology' consciously and decidedly moved into the tradition of modern philosophy but in such a way that 'transcendental subjectivity' attains a more original and universal determination through phenomenology. Phenomenology retained 'experiences of consciousness' as its thematic realm, but now in the systematically planned and secured investigation of the structure of acts of experience together with the investigation of the objects experienced in those acts with regard to their objectivity.

"In this universal project for a phenomenological philosophy, the *Logical Investigations,* too—which had so to speak remained philosophically neutral—could be assigned their systematic place. They were published in the same year (1913) in a second edition by the same publisher. Most of the investigations had in the meantime undergone 'profound revisions.' The sixth investigation, 'the most important with regard to phenomenology' (preface to the second edition) was, however, withheld. But the essay 'Philosophy as Exact Science' (1910–11) which Husserl contributed to the first volume of the new journal *Logos* also only now acquired a sufficient basis for its programmatical theses through the *Ideas.*

"Also in the year 1913, the publisher Max Niemeyer brought out the important study by Max Scheler: *On the Phenomenology of the Feelings of Sympathy and of Love and Hate, with an Appendix on the Reason for Assuming the Existence of Other Minds.*

". . . At that time the rather obvious idea was current that with 'phenomenology' a new school had arisen in European philosophy. Who could have denied the correctness of this statement?

"But such historical calculation did not comprehend what had happened in virtue of 'phenomenology,' that is, already with the *Logical Investigations.* This remained unspoken, and can hardly even be rightly expressed today. Husserl's own programmatical explanations and methodological presentations rather strengthened the misunderstanding that through 'phenomenology' a beginning of philosophy was claimed which denied all previous thinking.

"Even after the *Ideas* was published, I was still captivated by the never-ceasing spell of the *Logical Investigations.* That magic brought about anew an unrest unaware of its own reason, although it made one suspect that it came from the inability to attain the act of philosophical thinking called 'phenomenology' simply by reading the philosophical literature.

"My perplexity decreased slowly, my confusion dissolved laboriously, only after I met Husserl personally in his workshop.

"Husserl came to Freiburg in 1916 as Heinrich Rickert's successor. Rickert had taken over Windelband's chair in Heidelberg. Husserl's teaching took place in the form of a step-by-step training in phenomenological 'seeing' which at the same time demanded that one relinquish the untested use of philosophical knowledge. But it also demanded that one give up introducing the authority of the great thinkers into the conversation. However, the clearer it became to me that the increasing familiarity with phenomenological seeing was fruitful for the interpretation of Aristotle's writing, the less I could separate myself from Aristotle and the other Greek thinkers. Of course I could not immediately see what decisive consequences my renewed occupation with Aristotle was to have.

"As I myself practiced phenomenological seeing, teaching and learning in Husserl's proximity after 1919 and at the same time tried out a transformed understanding of Aristotle in a seminar, my interest leaned anew toward the *Logical Investigations*, above all the sixth investigation in the first edition. The distinction which is worked out there between sensuous and categorical intuition revealed itself to me in its scope for the determination of the 'manifold meaning of being.'

"For this reason we—friends and pupils—begged the master again and again to republish the sixth investigation which was then difficult to obtain. True to his dedication to the cause of phenomenology, the publisher Niemeyer published the last chapter of the *Logical Investigations* again in 1922. Husserl notes in the preface: 'As things stand, I had to give in to the wishes of the friends of this work and decide to make its last chapter available again in its old form.' With the phrase 'the friends of this work,' Husserl also wanted to say that he himself could not quite get close to the *Logical Investigations* after the publication of the *Ideas*. At the new place of his academic activity, the passion and

effort of his thought turned toward the systematic development of
the plan presented in the *Ideas* more than ever. Thus Husserl
could write in the preface mentioned to the sixth investigation:
'My teaching activity in Freiburg, too, furthered the direction of
my interest toward general problems and the system.'

"Thus Husserl watched me in a generous fashion, but at the
bottom in disagreement, as I worked on the *Logical Investigations*
every week in special seminars with advanced students in addition
to my lectures and regular seminars. Especially the preparation
for this work was fruitful for me. There I learned one thing—at
first rather led by surmise than guided by founded insight: What
occurs for the phenomenology of the acts of consciousness as the
self-manifestation of phenomena is thought more originally by
Aristotle and in all Greek thinking and existence as *aletheia*, as
the unconcealedness of what-is-present, its being revealed, its showing itself. That which phenomenological investigations rediscovered
as the supporting attitude of thought proves to be the fundamental
trait of Greek thinking, if not indeed of philosophy as such.

"The more decisively this insight became clear to me, the
more pressing the question became: Whence and how is it determined what must be experienced as 'the things themselves' in
accordance with the principle of phenomenology? Is it consciousness and its objectivity or is it the Being of beings in its unconcealedness and concealment?

"Thus I was brought to the path of the question of Being,
illumined by the phenomenological attitude, again made uneasy
in a different way than previously by the questions prompted by
Brentano's dissertation. But the path of questioning became longer
than I suspected. It demanded many stops, detours and wrong
paths. What the first lectures in Freiburg and then in Marburg
attempted shows the path only indirectly" (*On Time and Being*,
pp. 74–80).

This text has been quoted so extensively because it is one of
the few in which Heidegger speaks about his own development. It
is true that he did this in the context of an appreciation of
Niemeyer's services to phenomenology, but it also bears upon the

significance of phenomenology for Heidegger's own work and quest.[2]

Seen from the perspective of his entire teaching career, the Marburg period (1923–28) has been described by Heidegger as "the most stimulating, composed and eventful," a period which also includes the holidays which he always spent at his cottage in Todtnauberg. No lectures belonging precisely to this period have yet been published, though we do have, of course, *Being and Time, Kant and the Problem of Metaphysics, What is Metaphysics?*, and *The Essence of Reasons*. The beginnings of *Being and Time* can be traced back to the winter of 1923–24. That *Being and Time* contains the most significant impulses of his thinking since its very inception may well be taken for granted.[3]

Heidegger was appointed professor at Marburg especially on the recommendation of Paul Natorp, who had requisitioned for the faculty a manuscript by Heidegger, a manuscript dealing with his interpretation of Aristotle. Till the death of Natorp (1924), the two met almost every week, mostly on Wednesday afternoons, going together on silent walks in the neighboring forests. For both Natorp and Heidegger lived not so much in the exchange of argument as in the written, carefully thought-out word, in contrast with someone like Scheler, who shone in discussion. The frequently circulated view that Heidegger received the stimulus to write *Being and Time* from Protestant theology, in particular from Rudolf Bultmann, is without foundation. It would be truer to say, on the contrary, that it was theology that received a new impulse from Heidegger, a theology that was in the midst of a deep crisis.[4] Certainly the recommendation to appoint Heidegger did not come from the theologians.

In Marburg, friendship developed between Heidegger and Bultmann, and they sometimes attended each other's classes and had students in common. It was a lasting friendship. The philosopher Nicolai Hartmann was also in Marburg in this period. Heidegger, Hartmann, P. Friedländer, the archaeologist Jacobsthal and the church historian Hans von Soden had established a *Graeca* in which Homer, the tragic poets, Pindar and Thucydides were read. Hans Georg Gadamer correctly points out that this was the time when the Marburg school broke up because Neo-Kantianism had lost all influence.[5] It should perhaps be added that this was the time when the influence of phenomenology was spreading rapidly and when, as just indicated, Heidegger had given it a new turn. What Heidegger offered by way of phenomenological exercises had little to do with Husserl's analyses of constitution and reduction, but a great deal with his motto "To the things themselves." This concern for the "things themselves" was so effective in his interpretations that, through them, philosophers who seemed to have been long "obsolete" suddenly woke up to a new life, and their thinking was rendered so vividly present, and in such original fashion, that the effect was nothing short of revolutionary.[6] Specially worth mentioning for the Marburg period are the Plato and Aristotle interpretations. In the winter semester of 1924–25 Heidegger held a lecture course, four hours a week, on the dialogue *Sophist*. As an introduction, he provided an exegesis of Book VI of the *Nicomachean Ethics*, of which the focal point was the interpretation of ἀληϑεύειν (disclosing). Here, Aristotle expressly makes the subject of inquiry the different modes of being disclosed or revelatory, with a view to characterizing the highest, the most pre-eminent mode. An understanding of this book thus also opens up access to Aristotle's thought as a whole (see also *Being and Time*, footnote xlii (H.225) on p. 494 of the English translation).

1. Heidegger's mother as a young woman

2. The house where Heidegger was born

4. Heidegger as a schoolboy, about 1899

3. Heidegger's parents

5. Heidegger with his friend Blum, about 1906

6. Heidegger's junior high school class at the Berthold and Friedrich Gymnasium, 1907/1908. Heidegger is on the far right

7. Franz Brentano
(1838–1917)

8. Heidegger and his friend Schnerle
as high school students, 1909

9. Heinrich Rickert

10. Heidegger in the spring of 1912

11. Heidegger after his graduation, 1914

12. Edmund Husserl

13. Heidegger, about 1920

14. Max Scheler

15. Heidegger and his fiancée, Elfriede Petri, 1916

The Twofold Leitmotiv of Heidegger's Thinking: The Question about Being and the Question about Truth (Aletheia)

When we try to get to the core of Heidegger's questioning, to that in it which vivifies his thinking, which does not let his seeking come to rest, we come upon the astonishing fact that this core is in itself twofold. It is an inquiry into Being and at the same time an inquiry into *aletheia*. We cannot, here and now, fully grasp how this twofoldness is to be understood. It will be our task in this monograph, however, to investigate this doubling and to trace this interconnectedness in some of Heidegger's writings. We shall try to see how this happens, first in *Being and Time* (Chapter 4), then in "On the Essence of Truth" (Chapter 5), in "The Origin of the Work of Art" (Chapter 6), in the "Letter on 'Humanism' " (Chapter 7), in "The Question concerning Technology" (Chapter 8), in "The Nature of Language" (Chapter 9) and in "The End of Philosophy and the Task of Thinking" (Chapter 10).

By way of a preliminary elucidation of *aletheia*, a word may be offered in advance. *Aletheia* is translated by Heidegger as unhiddenness. It is a basic word in the Greeks' comprehension of Being. Any commerce with an entity* is possible only insofar as it is drawn out of hiddenness and has become unhidden. It is by no means

---

* *Das Seiende* has been rendered variously as "a being" or "beings," "an entity" or "entities," "what is" or "that which is," throughout this translation (Tr.).

through an act of judging that unhiddenness is first bestowed upon an entity. On the contrary, any statement can be made about an entity only insofar as it has already become unhidden. Unhiddenness is a feature of the entity itself. It is for this reason that Aristotle, for example, can equate unhidden, ἀληθές, and being, ὄν. A being is thought as what is present, in the sense of something that is stable and constant. This implies that it has a determinate form and fixed boundaries. That which is pre-eminently present in this sense is *physis*.

Man is the only being with the ability to perceive an entity in its unhiddenness, and this ability allows man to gather himself and concentrate on its unified character—λέγειν. Λέγειν means collecting, in the sense of gathering together. The *logos* makes this unified character manifest. In Greek experience, it is not man who occupies the central position, but that which is, a being, itself in its unhiddenness, to which man can admit himself by virtue of the *logos*, and to which he is capable of responding. At the same time, this *aletheia*, which sustains the Greek experience, is not, according to Heidegger, expressly subjected to thinking. We shall return to this later. It functions' like a horizon or boundary of vision, which renders an entity accessible to us; the less it explicitly stands out *as* a horizon, the better it can do so. It was therefore not at all necessary from the standpoint of the Greeks that *aletheia* should have become thematic or focal in the sense of being reflectively inquired about. On the other hand, it later became possible for *aletheia* itself to undergo a mutation in its nature. The clearest expression of this is to be found in the fact that "truth" was made dependent upon human apprehension.

As Heidegger himself says, his thinking has been set in motion, on the other hand, by the question about Being as it was suggested to him by the work of Brentano (see p. 9) and the "Ontology" of his teacher Braig. In what follows, we shall try to find out how the inquiry into *aletheia* and the inquiry into Being are related and how Heidegger arrives at the point of being able to think about this intimate connection. We shall also seek to explain why Heidegger's questioning leads back to the Greek experience and results in the course of metaphysics as such becoming the subject of inquiry.

The Question about Being in the Horizon of Time (Being and Time, 1927)

The following exposition of Heidegger's epoch-making work *Being and Time* is confined to four points: (1) its theme and arrangement; (2) Dasein as being-in-the-world; (3) the existentialia and temporality; (4) the problem of truth (§ 44).

It is not easy to reconstruct, after the event, the effect produced by the publication of *Being and Time*. Such an unusual work, in such independent language, was at first bound to appear strange to Heidegger's contemporaries. A series of time-honored, favorite problems of "classical" epistemology was simply swept aside by it. Even phenomenology, which was, after all, already a quarter of a century old, was suddenly given a novel definition—so novel that Husserl, to whom the work was dedicated, could not really comprehend it.

Husserl thought very highly of Heidegger and saw in him his most important pupil, one who would continue his work. Now he was suddenly disillusioned. This was not phenomenology as he conceived it. Heidegger saw in Husserl a renovator of the philosophy of the twentieth century and over and over again held seminars on the *Logical Investigations*, especially Investigation VI. But he was no disciple. On the contrary, he initiated a revolution in philosophical thinking for which Husserl was not at all prepared.

Although *Being and Time* was hardly understood (actually, because of the numerous misunderstandings, Heidegger himself wrote a pseudonymous critique of it, but then did not publish it), its influence began to spread increasingly, particularly among the younger generation. It became the most exciting text of our time and its impact, as Otto Pöggeler aptly remarks, "did not remain confined to the narrow circle of philosophers."[7]

All at once the whole set of problems in contemporary philosophy, from Neo-Kantianism to value-philosophy, became stale and, simultaneously, metaphysics from Plato to Nietzsche emerged in a new light. The customary separation of systematic and historical modes of inquiry became untenable, for the systematic method of inquiry can be grasped only in the context of history, being itself always historically conditioned.

ON THE SUBJECT MATTER AND ARRANGEMENT OF THE WORK

Being and Time is not a difficult work to read. Heidegger's language is clear, if one is prepared to listen to it. It proves to be more difficult, it is true, when we try to grasp the work in regard to its basic intention—to grasp, that is, the problem of the inner coherence of *Being and Time* as the central question. For that, it is necessary to have a clear idea of the general problem of Being, so that we may be in a position to understand why time can be described as the horizon for the question about Being. To be sure, there existed quite a number of investigations on time (to mention here only Bergson's and Husserl's), but the question of Being itself was not seen in all its trenchancy or even posed, despite the prevailing concern with all kinds of ontology. Heidegger himself has held back from publication his treatment of "Time and Being" (Part One, Division Three, p. 64*) and the work remained a torso. The missing parts were the most crucial. Most difficult of all is the task of understanding and interpreting retrospectively the unfold-

* Unless otherwise mentioned, page references in this chapter are to *Being and Time*, translated by John Macquarrie and Edward Robinson (New York: Harper & Row, 1962). In some cases, their translation has been modified.

ing of Heidegger's thinking from the perspective of its concluding phase, so that with the reading of this work we are challenged to move beyond it, annulling it as finally valid, and to subject it to a process of transformation, respectively. And this means at the same time to acquire insight into the necessity of the particular form it actually has. This has not been achieved so far, unless it be by Heidegger himself. The problem cannot be taken up in an introductory attempt such as this, though it must be mentioned here as a necessary task for the future. For, so long as we are unable to realize this, we cannot say that we understand Heidegger.

The very announcement of the question posed was bound to cause surprise—the problem about the sense of Being. Heidegger points out at the same time that this problem is by no means a new one. The quotation from Plato's *Sophist* ("For obviously you have long been familiar with what you mean when you use the expression 'being.' We, however, who once thought we understood it, have now become perplexed") is meant to remind us that the question is as old as metaphysics itself. Then, does Heidegger want to tie us down to tradition? By no means. He challenges the tradition, and he calls upon us to think this tradition through.

The following quotation places us right into the situation in question. "If the question about Being is to be explicitly formulated and carried through in such a manner as to be completely transparent to itself, then any treatment of it in line with the elucidations we have given requires us to explain how Being is to be looked at, how its meaning is to be understood and conceptually grasped; it requires us to prepare the way for choosing the right entity for our example, and to work out the genuine way of access to it. Looking at something, understanding and conceiving it, choosing, access to it—all these ways of behaving are constitutive for our inquiry, and therefore are modes of being for those particular entities which we, the inquirers, are ourselves. Thus to work out the question of Being adequately, we must make an entity—the inquirer—transparent in his own being. The very asking of this question is an entity's mode of *being*; and as such it gets its essential character from what is inquired about—namely, Being. This entity which each of us is himself and which includes inquiring as one of the possibilities of its being, we shall denote by the term 'Dasein.' If we are to formulate our question explicitly and transparently, we must first give a proper explication of an entity (Dasein), with regard to its being" (pp. 26–27).

From this passage in the text we see why the discussion of the question about Being begins with an analysis of the inquirer, or of Dasein. We cannot develop the question properly until we know what sort of being the questioner is. It is a being that is already marked by a certain understanding of Being. The discussion of this question does not carry us merely to the periphery of the theme of Being. On the contrary, it necessitates an elucidation of the particular mode of being of this entity—Dasein—as distinct from other entities—*vorhanden*, or present-at-hand, entities, and *zuhanden*, or ready-to-hand, entities. The distinctive character of the inquirer lies in the fact that he *is* not merely, but that for this entity, "in its very being, that being is an *issue* for it" (p. 32).

Heidegger's inquiry into the meaning of Being is presented as fundamental ontology. This fundamental ontology is not intended to work out a particularly comprehensive concept of Being but to offer an analysis of the mode of being of the inquirer—that is, of those basic structures which Heidegger calls "existentialia." The being of the inquirer is distinguished from all other entities by the fact that he builds up a certain relationship to himself. This ability to have an attitude toward oneself, to understand oneself in regard to the possibilities of one's being and indeed to be under the necessity of seizing hold of these, is the distinctive mark of an entity which is characterized by existence. "Existence" is a term employed exclusively for man. The structural determinations of man, the existentialia, are to be clearly distinguished from the basic determinations of entities other than men, which are called "categorial determinations" by Heidegger. This is a fundamental distinction. The nonhuman entity is, but it does not exist; for it, there is no possibility of having any relationship to itself.

What then is the twofold task involved in working out the question of Being? First, the analytic of Dasein, to be carried out here, and second, the destruction, or tearing down, of the history of ontology.

As to the first point: It is we ourselves who exist as Dasein. That we always move within a specific comprehension of Being appertains to our being itself. Hence, it appears to be particularly easy to state something about Dasein. That is an illusion. We succumb, on the contrary, to the temptation to understand ourselves in terms of the entity which we precisely *are not*, with which we relate ourselves invariably, in some fashion, as our "world." That which is of a non-Dasein character seduces us, by serving as the model for our understanding, into comprehending ourselves too according to its pattern. Man is better informed about what he has dealings with than about himself.

What is necessary is that we catch sight of Dasein itself as it is in the first instance and, thus, mostly in its everyday, common character. This satisfies the phenomenological requirement that we should not start out from any ideal image of man but grasp him in the mode of being in which he ordinarily is. But this is not to be done in such a way as to lose ourselves in the description of these modes of behavior and attitude, but in order to bring to light that which underlies this behavior, that is, the essential structures, or existentialia.

Heidegger sketches here a circular procedure: The analytic of Dasein is preliminary and is intended as an elaboration of the question of Being. When this is worked out, we have to come back with that in mind and repeat the analytic of Dasein. This happens in the second division, in which the existentialia are grasped afresh in the context of temporality (compare § 3). This is not just accidental, but is based rather on the fact that, according to Heidegger, temporality constitutes the horizon for understanding the being of Dasein. And this renders it necessary to think through again the problem of time as such. That, in turn, was to make it possible to conceive the temporality of Being itself—something that remains unaccomplished in the published part of *Being and Time*.

What does Heidegger mean by the "destruction of the history of ontology"? To begin with, we learn that Dasein itself is historical and that only because of this can there be such a thing as world history.

"Whatever the way of being it may have at the time, and

thus with whatever understanding of Being it may possess, Dasein has grown up both into and in a traditional way of interpreting itself: in terms of this it understands itself proximally and, within a certain range, constantly. By this understanding, the possibilities of being are disclosed and regulated. Its own past—and this always means the past of his 'generation'—is not something which *follows along after* Dasein, but something which already goes ahead of it" (p. 41).

This, however, seems to be in direct contradiction to the problem as it was formulated. In the case of average Dasein, the fact that Dasein is historical misleads it into falling back into the tradition. For, just as Dasein has the tendency to understand itself according to the model of what is other than Dasein, similarly, in its understanding of history, it has the tendency to succumb to tradition, to be guided by this tradition, to let itself derive its resolves and decisions from this tradition, without achieving clear insight into its specific historical reality.

What is veiled by the tradition has to be rendered accessible again. We have to understand with which specific concepts, coming down from which particular period, we operate, instead of acting as if we were dealing with a body of unchanging verities which we simply receive and then pass on. (This is explained and illustrated with reference to the history of ontology from antiquity to Kant and Hegel.)

Destroying the history of ontology means uncovering the historicity of its basic concepts, awakening the sense really for historicity, however paradoxical this may sound. But it also means uncovering all that has remained unnoticed in that which has been petrified in the tradition and handed down. The aim of destroying the petrified history of ontology is to make it transparent to us and to enable us to see and comprehend its limits. This has been Heidegger's lifelong concern, and it is in this sense that we have to understand his interpretations of Plato, Aristotle, Descartes, Leibniz, Kant, Fichte, Schelling, Hegel and Nietzsche, especially his interpretations of the early Greek thinkers.

What does Heidegger mean by the phenomenological method? He certainly does not just take over the specifically Husserlian phenomenology as a kind of transcendental philosophy. On the contrary, he puts the ahistorically conceived phenomenology of Husserl back into the historical context. Phenomenology understood as a methodological concept "does not characterize the what of the objects of philosophical research as subject-matter, but rather the *how* of that research" (p. 50).

It is not by chance that now, a quarter of a century after the inauguration of phenomenology as a new way of inquiry, it is itself subjected to an analysis which leads to a new determination of the concepts of *phenomenon* and *logos* (compare § 7, pp. 51–58). The concept of *phenomenon* is defined as "that which shows itself as itself," and *logos* is conceived as that which lets something be seen, which gives access to what is unhidden. That to which phenomenology is to give us access is now the *being* of beings. Thus, in this phase of his thinking, "*only as phenomenology, is ontology possible*" (p. 60). In relation·to Dasein, it emerges as hermeneutics in the sense of an explication of what appertains to Dasein, what happens in it. Such explication was also intended to provide the basis for all further ontological investigation. "Philosophy is universal phenomenological ontology, and takes its departure from the hermeneutic of Dasein, which, as an analytic of *existence*, has made fast the guiding-line for all philosophical inquiry at the point where it *arises* and to which it *returns*" (p. 62).

Heidegger had planned the work in two parts. The first part was to give the analytic of Dasein in the light of temporality, in order to show how time constitutes the horizon for the question of Being. In the second part, the destruction of the history of ontology was to be carried out and illustrated in respect to the problematic of temporality.

The first part was planned in three divisions: (1) the preparatory fundamental analysis of Dasein; (2) Dasein and temporality; (3) time and Being. The second part was to contain: (1) Kant's doctrine of Schematism in the context of the problematic of temporality; (2) the ontological foundation of the *cogito sum* of Descartes and the taking over of medieval ontology within the problematic of the *res cogitans*; (3) a discussion of Aristotle's treatise on time, in order to exhibit the limits of ancient ontology as they become visible in this treatise.

Only the first and second divisions of the first part were published. The dean of the Faculty of Philosophy at Marburg had pressed Heidegger to publish because the faculty had recommended Heidegger *unico loco* as Nicolai Hartmann's successor to the Ministry, and the Ministry wanted a publication (see *On Time and Being*, p. 80). The third division was held back by Heidegger because, as he put it, he had not yet found the language adequate to this way of thinking.

As for the second part, the portion containing the interpretation of Kant appeared independently in the volume *Kant and the Problem of Metaphysics*.[8]

DASEIN AS BEING-IN-THE-WORLD

The traditional ways of speaking about man in terms of consciousness—subject, I and the like—are absent in *Being and Time*. The term "Dasein," that is, being-there, is used instead. It must be admitted, though, that this way of putting it is misleading. It is not a matter of substituting one expression for another and leaving everything else as it was. On the contrary, the change in terminology signifies a change in the way of seeing, of comprehending and, hence, of thinking. The term "Dasein" is meant to announce that here man is regarded from a specific point of view, as a being who is distinguished by his relationship to Being.

What is Being? We do not know that. What we can see easily, however, is that among the entities known to us, there is a distinction between the entity which can develop a relationship to itself and the entity which is incapable of doing so. A stone is, but it has no relationship to itself and cannot have any attitude toward itself. The same is true of a tree, a chair and all other nonhuman entities. Man not only is, but he develops a relationship to himself as well as a relationship to his fellow men and to nonhuman entities. This has important consequences. Man is, but beyond that, he has to be; his being is a task imposed on him.

Here we have a preliminary signification of Being, namely,

Being in the sense of the specific being of man. And this specific being is taken, not as that which simply is, but as something that is to be realized, which Heidegger summarizes in the expression "to-be" (it has to be) as an attribute of Dasein. Dasein is an entity to which its being is committed as a task. However, this insight by no means entitles us to conclude that we now know what Being means. We are on the way to describing the being of one particular sort of entity.

To say that Dasein relates itself to its own being is to define its being as existence. "And because we cannot define Dasein's essence by citing a 'what' of the kind that pertains to a subject-matter, and because its essence lies rather in the fact that in each case it has its being to be, and has it as its own, we have chosen to designate this entity as 'Dasein', a term which is purely an expression of its being" (pp. 32–33). It is in its specific mode of being that its distinctive character lies, and this specific mode consists in the fact that it can choose itself, indeed must choose itself, for not choosing is also a kind of choice (an idea that was taken over by Sartre and plays an important role in his thought). In this lies the origin of the central distinction between authenticity and inauthenticity. "Dasein always understands itself in terms of its existence—in terms of a possibility of itself: to be itself or not itself. Dasein has either chosen these possibilities itself, or got itself into them, or grown up in them already. Only the particular Dasein decides its existence, whether it does so by way of taking hold or by neglecting" (p. 33).

The choice can ensue in such a manner that by it, and in it, Dasein attains to itself, realizes its own inmost possibilities, or in a manner that Dasein lets the choice be, as it were, pregiven to it and thus exists in the mode dictated by the "they." This is equivalent to inauthenticity.

We said above that the peculiar character of Dasein lies in the fact that its being manifests itself in existing, indeed that it realizes itself in existing. This definition is further elucidated by the term "my-ownness," which means that for each entity having this mode of being it is a question of its own being, not just a matter of any general mode of being.

"And because Dasein is in each case essentially its own possibility, it *can*, in its very being, 'choose' itself and win itself; it can also lose itself and never win itself; or only 'seem' to do so. But only in so far as it is essentially something which can be *authentic*—that is, something of its own—can it have lost itself and not yet won itself. As modes of being, *authenticity* and *inauthenticity* . . . are both grounded in the fact that any Dasein whatsoever is characterized by mineness" (p. 68).

In authenticity, Dasein chooses those possibilities through which it attains itself; in inauthenticity, it lets the possibilities be laid down in advance by others, or be determined by the anonymity of the "they." "They" engage in sport, "they" study law, "everybody" goes to a particular holiday resort, "one" marries within a certain milieu, "one" favors a particular political party and so on.

What should be the starting point of the analysis of Dasein? Heidegger finds this in averageness and everydayness—in the mode of being which we come across in the first instance and mostly, or in the mode of being in which we ourselves are, mostly and to begin with. It is in this average Dasein that we find those structures which are valid for every Dasein, authentic as well as inauthentic.

This preliminary account should enable us to take the next step of conceptualizing Dasein as *being-in-the-world*. The difficulty here lies in the fact that a complex structure is to be described as a unified phenomenon, which can only be done piecemeal, so to speak, yet without losing sight of the unity which underlies the analysis and on the basis of which it is developed.

Being-in-the-world is explained in three steps: (1) by inquiring into what "world" means here; (2) by the inquiry into the *who*, that is, into Dasein in its averageness as being-with and being-itself; (3) by asking what being-in means, which includes an examination of the structural elements, or existentialia.

In order to get the inquiry into being-in-the-world on the right track, it is essential to provide a brief preliminary elucidation of being-in. We usually think about being-in in terms of the sphere of things. There it means being-contained-in. But if Dasein cannot be conceived as a thinglike entity or as something simply present-at-hand, being-in also must be interpreted in a different way.

Being-in is meant to be taken as an existential, in the sense of being familiar-with. What I am familiar with is something I dwell on. Being-in cannot be regarded as being spatially contained in something. This, however, does not mean that Dasein has no specific relation to space, though this is a relation to which we cannot gain access so long as we approach it in terms of the spatial relation of one thing being contained in another. Also, it is by no means the case that only by first analyzing the phenomenon of knowing can we arrive at the notion of being-in. On the contrary, it is only because we are already familiar with entities—a relationship which is expressed in the most diverse modes of concern or caring—that we have the capability for a specific mode of cognition, namely, that of knowing.

Without becoming apparent at first, this leads to a reversal of the prevailing view, according to which knowing constitutes the foundation of every sort of commerce with things. Only because we dwell on or linger over an entity with which we are in some way acquainted, which is at our disposal, which we need and the like, is it possible for us, by adopting a special attitude, to leave behind the attitude of having a practical concern with it, to refrain from such concern and regard it in a purely contemplative manner. The latter attitude is by no means primary. This also implies that a merely epistemological starting point always leaves out of account its own foundation. The primacy of mere knowing is an illusion of the epistemologist. This does not mean that Heidegger intends to relinquish knowledge as such, but only that he seeks to reach down to a deeper foundation from where it can be seen that in pure knowing there is implied something like a shutting out of view of that relation of familiar commerce which knowing always presupposes. In other words, knowing is also a mode of being-with, though one in which the usual practical relationship to entities is disregarded.

This leads to the heart of an old problem, namely, the question as to how the subject can step out of its inner sphere in order to reach the object "out there." Heidegger cuts this Gordian knot by starting from the principle that Dasein, as being-in-the-world, is always already out there—with the familiar world.

"When Dasein directs itself towards something and grasps it, it does not somehow first get out of an inner sphere in which it has been proximally encapsulated, but its primary kind of being is such that it is always 'outside,' alongside entities which it encounters and which belong to a world already discovered. . . . And furthermore, the perceiving of what is known is not a process of returning with one's booty to the 'cabinet' of consciousness after one has gone out and grasped it; even in perceiving, retaining, and preserving, the Dasein which knows *remains outside*, and it does so *as Dasein*" (p. 89).

It is not through the agency of knowing that the production of a relation to the world is made possible. Knowing always presupposes this relation and is simply a transformation of that relation; "in knowing, Dasein achieves a new *status of being* towards a world which has already been discovered in Dasein itself. . . . But a *'commercium'* of the subject with a world does not get *created* for the first time by knowing, nor does it *arise* from some way in which the world acts upon a subject. Knowing is a mode of Dasein founded upon being-in-the-world" (p. 90). This is a revolution in the way of thinking, to speak with Kant, which has dismayed some of Heidegger's contemporaries and which others have acclaimed with enthusiasm.

In order to understand the meaning of being-in-the-world, we must first examine what "world" means. We cannot explain this if we begin by adducing examples of things within the world. By stringing together a series of entities within the world, we can never arrive at anything like a world. We may classify entities into various categories such as man, things made by man, natural things and value-charged things, then trace them back to their ultimate foundation in Nature and arrive at a scientific determination of Nature itself. But even then we do not get any further. "Nature is itself an entity which is encountered within the world and which can be discovered in various ways and at various stages" (p. 92).

How then should we proceed? Heidegger takes the radical step of turning the whole question around, so that worldliness or worldhood is to be understood as a constitutive element of Dasein, that is, as an existential. "Ontologically, 'world' is not a way of characterizing those entities which Dasein essentially is *not;* it is rather a characteristic of Dasein itself" (p. 92).

This seems to relegate the world to the sphere of the subjective. But why then has Heidegger almost totally ruled out the concept of the subjective? How can we get closer to the meaning of world and of worldliness? According to the directive we met with earlier, we should take the average Dasein in its everyday character as our starting point. The world of such Dasein is the environing world, the world of its surroundings. The path to be followed is quite clearly indicated: "That world of everyday Dasein which is closest to it, is the *environment.* From this existential character of average being-in-the-world, our investigation will take its course from the idea of worldhood in general. We shall seek the worldhood of the environment (environmentality) by going through an ontological interpretation of those entities within-the-*environment* which we encounter as closest to us" (p. 94).

Heidegger's analysis of utensils (*Zeug,* gear or equipment) is among the best-known passages of *Being and Time.* What is not equally well known is the import of this analysis. Obviously, it cannot be a matter of giving directives about how man should deal with articles of use in his environing world, for such dealings are something with which we are most intimately familiar. As we grow up in our world, we grow into men capable of such dealings. This analysis is also not concerned with showing how working with these implements can bring about a change in the world or actually even alienate it from man. The aim of the analysis is to make us understand how much prior knowledge and close familiarity must already be there before anything can become accessible to Dasein as a utensil, and how such prior knowledge is not given here in a theoretical attitude. One of the insights of this analysis is the discovery that our way of dealing with utensils has its own "sight" and that we fail to have in our grasp what is typically utensillike if we start out with a purely theoretical mode of viewing things.

Let us take a simple example. I have a hammer in front of me and I try to describe it in a theoretical attitude—it is so big, of such a color, of this form, of such weight, made of such and such material and so on. But in doing so, I fail to grasp just what this implement is for, the fact that it is something to hammer with. Whether it holds well in the hand, is not too heavy and the like, that is something I cannot understand by pure observation but only in the course of handling and using it. Every utensil is a utensil for doing something. Handling an implement means subordinating oneself to the specific "in order to" in every case. Heidegger calls the specific mode of being of a utensil "ready-to-handness" or "handiness." This is nothing else but the explicit formulation of something that we experience every day without articulating it in words.

The characteristic sight that guides our manipulative dealings is circumspection (*Umsicht*). As stated already, the purely theoretical way of seeing is by no means the primary one. Rather, in order to arrive at the purely theoretical attitude, we must abandon, jump out of, the specific circumspect way of seeing. This is important if we are to account for what is no longer apprehended as a result of this jumping out. It should be clearly seen that we do not start out with a simply present-at-hand entity lying before us and then, by adding to it value attributes and the like, arrive at a ready-to-hand entity. The universally current view, which begins by conceiving a thing as *res extensa* and then grafts upon the *extensio* all kinds of attributes, is simply erroneous. The ready-to-hand entity is what we find most immediately given in our environing world; it is through it that we find our way about and secure our needs in life.

Let us have a closer look at the utensil. As we stated earlier, every utensil is a utensil for something. "The work to be produced, as the 'what-for' of the hammer, the plane and the needle, has in turn the mode of being of a utensil. The shoe which is to be made is for wearing, the clock is manufactured for telling time. The product which is encountered in our concernful dealings—which we find in the course of our work—lets us encounter at the same time the 'what-for' of its usability, for this usability is essentially part of it. The completed work, in turn, is there only by reason of its use and of the referential context of entities which is discovered in this use" (p. 99).

We have, in addition, the fact that production implies utilizing something, namely, that *from which* the thing is produced. This refers us to Nature as the source of this "from-which." Finally, producing also directs our attention to that *for whom* something is made.

What has this analysis of utensils to do with the problem of the worldhood of the world, thus with the problem of what it is that makes a world into a world? Heidegger shows this by means of examples in which the utensil appears precisely to give up its implemental character. It is when the utensil becomes unusable (conspicuousness), or when it is missing (obtrusiveness) or when it lies in our way (obduracy) that we are led to see how the utensil is determined by its referential character. It is precisely when the "in order to . . . for that purpose" reference is disturbed (for example, when I do not find the hammer with which to drive the nail) that it expressly comes into view as reference. "The context of equipment is lit up, not as something never seen before, but as a totality constantly sighted beforehand in circumspection. With this totality, however, the world announces itself" (p. 105). In order for the world to be lit up, it must already be opened up or disclosed. This is explained by analyzing, as an example, a particular utensil, namely the sign. The peculiar thing about a utensil is that through it a context of utensils is expressly brought into view (for instance, a traffic sign and the context of the behavior of those in the traffic). The ordinary utensil (say, a pen) is inconspicuous because it directs the attention of the person using it, not toward itself but toward the task at hand (the article or book to be written). The sign as a utensil, on the contrary, is quite conspicuous, which is just what enables it to make the reference explicit. It is by means of the specific signs that the particular environing world, to which they then belong, is expressly rendered accessible.

What defines a utensil is its serviceableness. The latter is concretized in a utensil by virtue of the fact that the context in which the utensil stands, and to which it belongs, is specifically made visible here, as also the environing world of which this context is itself a part.

The specific character of the world as such, however, still

remains to be explained. This is done in § 18. That a utensil is defined in terms of reference means "it has the character that *with* it a certain end is reached—its function terminates *in* something. The ontological character of an at-hand entity is such destination [*Bewandtnis*]. Destination implies letting something reach its goal in something" (p. 115).

The utensil is always seen in the light of the destination that is constitutive of it. There is no such thing as a utensil taken by itself. A utensil always exists in a context of utensils, within a totality of utensils. What a utensil is destined for is something that is predetermined by the totality of destinations (for example, a tool to a workshop). The totality of destinations has its final point of reference in Dasein; it is for the sake of Dasein. As Heidegger formulates it, "this primary for-what is not just a for-it regarded as a possible point of destination [*Wobei einer Bewandtnis*]. The primary for-what is a for-the-sake-of-which" (p. 116).

In these analyses Heidegger shows what sort of knowledge Dasein must already have in order that anything like a utensil may be encountered by it, and that Dasein must have this knowledge in a peculiarly prethematic manner. What we have here is a straight bit of analysis in the sense of laying bare a constitutive *a priori*, which is not, however, an epistemological *a priori* but rather an *a priori* for just the immediate dealings we have with things. The analysis exhibits the world as that which must be opened up already in order for intramundane entities like utensils to be encountered (cf. p. 86).

Heidegger, thus, does not construct, but rather takes the concrete phenomenon as his starting point and lays open all its implications for the possibility of man's handling of utensils. The references within which Dasein moves presuppose that it has projected itself upon particular possibilities, through which these entities can be encountered by it in particular ways. Heidegger's definition of world runs as follows:

"*The wherein of the referential comprehension, as that in view of which* [*woraufhin*] *the encounter with entities is made possible in the mode of being proper to destination, is the phenomenon of world*" (p. 119).⁹

It is the worldhood of the world that enables Dasein to experience entities such as utensils. This means that world is a particular mode of understanding, an existential, a fundamental property of Dasein, which enables it to apprehend entities in its
environment in their specific usability, to be acquainted with them
but not grasping them in a theoretical manner. It is clear now
that being-in-the-world cannot mean being present as one particular entity among others. It means, rather, developing something like a world-comprehension, through which entities become
available to Dasein. This is by no means a subjectivization of the
world-concept but only a consistent formulation of the fact that
world is something in the nature of a basic comprehension and
thus part of Dasein's constitution. Heidegger next goes on to
contrast this world-understanding with the Cartesian definition of
world as *res extensa* and to trace this Cartesian definition to traditional ontology.

But if the Cartesian concept of the world as *res extensa* is
rejected, what are we to think of the spatiality of the world?

What is the spatial significance of handiness? It is nearness
(*Nähe*). We must not think of nearness or closeness in terms of
geometrically measurable distance, in the Cartesian manner. That
as such is not relevant to our everyday dealings with utensils, for
these dealings are governed by caring, or concern [*Besorgen*]. It is
on the basis of concern that a direction is fixed in which utensils
become available to us.

What is essential to a utensil is not an abstract position in
space—in a homogeneous, leveled space—but the fact that it has its
own determinate *place*. Part of being a utensil is that it should be
assigned a specific position and be available there for use from
time to time. From the place in which it is located we can often
infer what purpose the utensil serves. The utensil-totality, in turn,
is formed by assigning a different place to each utensil making up
this totality. The point is that the places cannot be arbitrarily ex-
changed, for each place is allotted to a utensil just because it is this
particular utensil and is required for this particular activity. Its
place is that point in space where the utensil belongs.

The assignment of a particular place for a particular utensil is preceded by some sort of acquaintance with the region. The region contains the unity of a utensil-context and, thus, of an articulated place-manifold. "Something like a region must first be discovered if there is to be any possibility of allotting or coming across places for a totality of equipment that is circumspectively at one's disposal" (p. 136).

What is important in terms of Heidegger's concern here is that we have not first given a three-dimensional manifold of possible positions, which is then furnished or filled up with things present-at-hand. On the contrary, space has become available by way of the familiar region, within which the utensil-manifolds are fitted up. In the environing world we have space in the mode of an organization of places which obtain their orientation from what we do and from what we intend to accomplish in life. So much for the spatiality of entities at hand. What constitutes the specific spatiality of Dasein itself? It lies in apartness (*Entfernung*) and situating (*Ausrichtung*). A-partness (*Ent-fernung*) should not be understood in the static sense of two things lying far apart, or as a certain distance between them which remains fixed. It should be understood in an active, transitive sense, as de-distancing, or causing the farness (*Ferne*, remoteness) to disappear. Dasein lets entities be encountered in nearness or closeness to us. It is by bringing close, causing the remoteness to disappear (*Ent-fernen*), that spatial distance (*Entferntheit*) is discovered. De-distancing is an existential determination—something brought about by Dasein; distance is a categorial one—the spatial distance between things.

In de-distancing, Dasein seeks what it needs most, to have something to-hand. Moreover, it can hardly be denied that such de-distancing is a characteristic of our times, that everything we do is designed to abolish and overcome remoteness (ever-faster transportation, transmission of news and the like). What lies at the back of this attitude is a question that is not taken up in the present context but is dealt with thoroughly in the later writings (compare Chapter 8).

Let us now try to consider Dasein in a way that will enable us to grasp what Heidegger calls *being-with* and *being-one's-self*. Heidegger commenced his analysis of being-in-the-world with an examination of utensils because "proximally and for the most part

Dasein is fascinated with its world. Dasein is thus absorbed in
[*benommen*] the world" (p. 149). Proceeding further, we see that
we do not have, to begin with, just the I, for which then its world
must be found and to which it must transcend. Similarly, there is
no such thing as an isolated ego, of which the isolation has to be
overcome by establishing a relation with the other. Even in the
account of the environing world, the other was thought of as being
copresent, for when anything is produced it is meant for somebody.
The tool is so made that others can use it. The others are also
copresent. They are not alien to us but precisely those with whom
we are together, from whom we do not distinguish ourselves. "The
world of Dasein is a world-with [*Mitwelt*]. Being-in is *being-with*
others. Their being-in-themselves within-the-world is Dasein-with"
(p. 155).

Saying that Dasein is Dasein-with is meant to make just this
point clear. It does not mean that as a matter of actual fact there
are always other men present in my neighborhood, but that I am
ever opened up for others, am along with others. Even when I
isolate myself and withdraw into solitude, I can do so only because my being is a being-with. When one avoids the presence of
one's fellow man, he is nevertheless, in such avoidance, present as
one who is avoided.

Just as our mode of dealing with utensils was described as
concern, our association with others is conceived as solicitude
(*Fürsorge*). This expression, taken as an existential, is used in such
a comprehensive sense that it includes all modes of being with
others, from love and self-sacrifice to indifference and contempt
for others. The latter, of course, is a deficient mode of solicitude.

In positive solicitude, Heidegger distinguishes between two
extreme possibilities: the jumping-in and the jumping-ahead solicitude. In the jumping-in type, one takes away, so to speak, the
burden of one's fellow man; here, the latter is in danger of becoming enslaved and dependent. In the jumping-ahead type, the
intention is to give back, so to speak, the care to the cared-for
person, so that he may be able to bear it himself. The "sight"
(*Sicht*) proper to solicitude is considerateness (*Rücksicht*) and
forbearance (*Nachsicht*).

We must now consider the question of the "who" of being-together-with. Since Heidegger's starting point is from the everyday mode of being of Dasein, the "who" of everyday being-together-with is exhibited as the "they," or Everyman—that is to say, man in his averageness. "The 'they', in its being, essentially makes an issue of this. Thus the 'they' maintains itself in fact in the averageness of that which is proper, of that which it regards as valid and that which it does not, and of that to which it grants success and that to which it denies it. In this averageness with which it prescribes what can and may be ventured, it keeps watch over everything exceptional that thrusts itself to the fore. Every kind of priority gets noiselessly suppressed. . . . This care of averageness reveals in turn an essential tendency of Dasein which we call the 'levelling down' of all possibilities of Being" (pp. 164–65). The form of being of the "they" is based on disburdening or exonerating oneself, for it is not the individual, but Everyman, who has to accept responsibility for all decisions. One notices in this a strange camouflage. The sovereignty of Everyman is a sovereignty that conceals itself. Everyone acts as if he were himself, while no one is actually his own self. Heidegger contrasts the lack of independence and inauthenticity of this manner of existing with authenticity, in which Dasein chooses itself on the basis of its very own possibilities. That there can be situations in which such a choice is greatly curtailed because of external limitations, though not expressly discussed by Heidegger, is adequately taken into account, however, in the concept of "being thrown."

The domination of the "they" also determines the manner of understanding world and oneself. Because Everyman has forfeited himself to his world (the world of the "they"), it is not surprising that he should understand himself then according to the model of a non-Dasein type of being, which in turn is something that traditional ontology, with its mistaken premise, enables us to understand.

The analysis of being-in-the-world includes an explicit clarification of being-in, that is, of the constitutive factors which give us access to Dasein regarded as overtness. These are disposition, or state-of-mind (*Befindlichkeit*), understanding and speech.

"In a state-of-mind Dasein is always brought before itself, and has already found itself, not in the sense of coming across itself by perceiving itself, but in the sense of finding itself in the mood that it has" (p. 174).

What was commonly overlooked or misunderstood—indeed, actually suppressed—in the philosophical view of man which was based on a particular concept of rationality, which was regarded as exemplary, is the immediately revelatory function of attunement. Let us take a simple example. We become acquainted with a man. Our first reaction is determined by the attunement or mood (*Stimmung*) which his presence near us evokes. This general feeling may undergo changes in the course of a longer time spent in his company, or it may alter suddenly. But this does not diminish the significance of moods as a primary mode of being open. The revelatory character of dispositions is the exciting thing about this phenomenon, which cannot be grasped, however, so long as moods are understood merely as a kind of "psychical coloring" constituting the "irrational" part of the psyche. When we speak in this manner, we deliberately make ourselves blind to what the phenomenon shows us, the fact that it is indeed through moods that our primary encounter with others, with the surrounding world and even with ourselves takes place.

"*The mood has already disclosed, in every case, being-in-the-world as a whole, and makes it possible first of all to direct oneself towards something.* Having a mood is not related to the psychical in the first instance, and is not itself an inner condition which then reaches forth in an enigmatical way and puts its mark on things and persons. It is in this that the *second* essential characteristic of states-of-mind shows itself. We have seen that the world, Dasein-with, and existence are *equiprimordially disclosed,* and state-of-mind is a basic existential species of their disclosedness, because this disclosedness itself is essentially being-in-the-world" (p. 176).

For Heidegger, attunement or mood has in addition the function of giving to Dasein itself access to its aspect of thrownness, the fact that it is, "the facticity of being delivered up" (p. 135). And lastly, as we have it in the most comprehensive definition, "Dasein's openness to the world is constituted existentially by the attunement of a state-of-mind" (p. 176).

Let us clarify this with an example: I can perceive something in my world as threatening me only because I am capable of experiencing fear. Attunement is thus by no means a phenomenon limited merely to the subject and his perceptions, but is a mode of being open by which the world can become accessible in the most diverse ways—as threatening, delightful, welcome, exciting and so on. In every disposition, I already have some knowledge about myself. Heidegger's analysis of moods has also influenced psychiatry, to mention here only the work of Ludwig Binswanger. Heidegger refers to the line of thinkers, from Augustine and Pascal down to Scheler, for whom the significance of attunement was in some way already recognized.

The second structural component is *understanding*. Disposition and understanding are equioriginal. In disposition also, understanding was already involved, for, as we said, every way of being attuned is directly revelatory. By the way, understanding is taken here not as a concept opposite to that of explaining but as a fundamental mode of Dasein. The specific interpretation of understanding as an existential of Dasein brings to light its projective character.

"In understanding, as an *existentiale*, that which we have such competence over is not a 'what', but being as existing. The kind of being which Dasein has, as potentiality-for-being, lies existentially in understanding" (p. 183).

The connection between understanding and possibility is very clearly stated in the following text. "As a mode of disclosure, understanding always pertains to the entire underlying structure of being-in-the-world. Not only is the world, *qua* world, revealed as possible significance, but the setting free of entities within the world itself is at the same time releasing them for *their* possibilities. The handy entity is discovered as such in its service*ability*, us*ability* and injurious*ness*. The totality of destinations is revealed as the categorical whole of a *possibility* of the coherent system of ready-to-hand entities. But even the 'unity' of the manifold of present-at-hand entities, Nature, is discoverable only by virtue of a *possibility* of it being disclosed" (pp. 144–45).

To the question of why understanding is always set on possibilities, why it moves within the dimension of possibilities, Heidegger replies, "because the understanding has in itself the existential structure which we call *'projection'* " (pp. 184–85). In understanding, Dasein opens up its own space for the free play of its existence as well as the free space for the play of entities which become available to it within the world. The two go together. The understanding which arises out of one's own self and is in accord with it, is called by Heidegger authentic; understanding which conceives Dasein in terms of the world is called inauthentic. The authentic and inauthentic ways of understanding may in turn be genuine or spurious. Thus, there may be an understanding of world which Dasein develops originally, in which case it is genuine; or it may develop it within a framework already given, without putting it into question and without actually understanding it, in which case it is spurious.

While explaining the utensil-world, we mentioned a specific "sight"—circumspection—and in connection with being-with, we spoke of considerateness. Now, understanding itself is defined as "sight" (*Sicht*). It is because understanding is primarily a kind of seeing that Dasein can display the various modes of sight involved in the circumspection of concern and the considerateness of solicitude. The sight directed at existence itself is called the "seeing-through sight," or transparency (*Durchsichtigkeit*). The modes of sight mentioned above are included in, are indeed rendered possible by, this transparent seeing. Because Dasein is constituted by understanding, it is capable of having some knowledge, not only of itself but also of the world and the others. We should at the same time bear in mind also that the term "sight" is meant to signify the fact that Dasein "lets entities which are accessible to it be encountered unconcealedly in themselves" (p. 187). What is involved in such sight is the character of openness or "clearedness" (*Gelichtetheit*) proper to Dasein.

Understanding is Dasein's mode of being as openness, for in understanding it projects itself on the possibilities of its ability-to-be. No projecting, however, occurs in a vacuum; as ability-to-be, it is already delivered up to thrownness, that is, to what is also termed "facticity." My project, for example, must reckon with a given talent and with my limitations, for otherwise it runs the risk of becoming illusory or of leading to self-deception.

In his analysis of understanding, Heidegger differentiates between understanding as interpretation (*Auslegung*) and understanding as statement. "The projecting of the understanding has its own inherent possibility—that of developing itself. This development of the understanding we call 'interpretation'. In it the understanding appropriates understandingly that which is understood by it" (p. 188). Interpretation is not the mere "acquiring of information about what is understood; it is rather the working-out of possibilities projected in understanding" (pp. 188–89).

From the analysis of the example of world-understanding given in § 32, let us pick out only a few points. In the understanding of a utensil as an "implement for," the peculiar feature to be noticed is the "as-structure." "That which is disclosed in understanding—that which is understood—is already accessible in such a way that its 'as which' can be made to stand out explicitly. The 'as' makes up the structure of the explicitness of something that is understood. It constitutes the interpretation" (p. 189). This should be kept in mind as a safeguard against the view that understanding is something that takes place only with a statement.

Pre-possession (*Vorhabe*, fore-having), pre-view (*Vorsicht*, fore-sight) and pre-conception (*Vorgriff*, fore-conception) are the three constitutive elements of our immediate comprehension of world in its character as environing us. A utensil is comprehended by us in terms of the totality of destination, the purposive whole, in which it is embedded. Underlying this is our attitude of having something to do, which in turn depends on our ability-to-be (project). The specific manner in which we approach an entity is called by Heidegger "pre-view," or "fore-sight." This does not have the meaning of proceeding cautiously, but the projective anticipation in which all our dealings are embedded.

"Anything understood which is held in our fore-having and towards which we set our sights 'foresightedly', becomes conceptualizable through the interpretation" (p. 191). The way in which Dasein has decided to conceive this thing in explicating it is the "pre-conception." It is not by chance that the prefixes "pre-" or "fore-" occur in all these terms. It has reference to the subsequent discussion of temporality, where it is shown how, in projecting, some kind of temporalizing of the future is in play. In this context Heidegger offers an elucidation of what he means by "meaning," or "sense" (*Sinn*).

"The *concept of meaning* embraces the formal existential framework of what necessarily belongs to that which an understanding interpretation articulates. *Meaning is the 'upon-which' of a projection in terms of which something becomes intelligible as something; it gets its structure from a fore-having, a fore-sight, and a fore-conception*" (p. 193). And in all consistency, sense must correspondingly be understood as something that belongs to Dasein. "Meaning is an *existentiale* of Dasein, not a property attaching to entities, lying 'behind' them, or floating somewhere as an 'intermediate domain'. Dasein only 'has' meaning, so far as the disclosedness of being-in-the-world can be 'filled in' by the entities discoverable in that disclosedness. *Hence only Dasein can be meaningful or meaningless*" (p. 193).

Heidegger set forth speech as the third existential of Dasein. What does he mean by "speech," or "discourse"?

"*Discourse is equiprimordial with state-of-mind and understanding*. The intelligibility of something has always been articulated, even before there is any appropriative interpretation of it. Discourse is the articulation of intelligibility. Therefore, it underlies both interpretation and assertion" (pp. 203–4). Furthermore, "the intelligibility of being-in-the-world—an intelligibility which goes with a state-of-mind—*expresses itself as discourse*. The totality-of-significations of intelligibility is *put into words*. To significations, words accrue. But word-things do not get supplied with significations" (p. 204). The concept of communication (*Mitteilung*) has a broad meaning: "Through it a co-state-of-mind [*Mitbefindlichkeit*] gets 'shared', and so does the understanding of being-with [*Mitsein*]" (p. 205). Because Dasein is being-with, it always stands within a certain sharing-together—for it exists always in a certain comprehending-together and being-disposed-together. For this reason, that speaking is most intelligible in which a community of disposition, or state-of-mind, and understanding is already present and does not have to be produced subsequently.

The utterance that takes place in speech does not mean the

self-expression of something inside us. On the contrary, Dasein is always already out there and articulates what is experienced there. "In discourse the intelligibility of being-in-the-world (an intelligibility which goes with a state-of-mind) is articulated according to significations; and discourse is this articulation" (p. 206). Heidegger points out that, in this connection, linguistic science must be placed on ontologically deeper foundations and freed from its domination by a specific concept of logic.

THE EXISTENTIALIA AND TEMPORALITY

The analysis of Dasein must accomplish a double task. It must lay out the separate elements of being-in-the-world, and it must exhibit the unity and interconnectedness of these elements. This second step needs to be described now. Heidegger takes this step by way of defining the basic structure of Dasein as *care*. This also means repeating the analysis of Dasein in the light of temporalization.

The three characteristics of Dasein we encountered are *existentiality* (Dasein is from the very first moved by its ability-to-be, which it has to realize), *facticity* (Dasein is ever already determined by that in the midst of which it is "thrown," which does not depend on it, which it has to take over) and *being forfeited* (it understands itself in terms of just that which it is not and abandons itself to the realm of entities familiar to it). These three characteristics are combined in *care*. Care does not mean being anxious or depressed. It is to be taken rather as encompassing a threefold structure: being-ahead-of-itself (existentiality), in already-being-in (facticity) as being-beside (being forfeited). The inquiry into the unity of this triad remains to be pursued further. This is done in the second division of the work, entitled "Dasein and Temporality."

"If the interpretation of Dasein's being is to become primordial, as a foundation for working out the basic question of ontology, then it must first have brought to light existentially the being of

Dasein in its possibilities of *authenticity* and *totality*" (p. 276).

In order to comprehend the ability-to-be-whole, the analysis must also include within its scope the end of Dasein. This end is death. Existentially, death is experienced as being-toward-death. This is the theme of the first chapter of this division. This is followed by an examination of the problem about the authenticity of existing, namely, conscience (Chapter 2). The call of conscience "gives no information about world-events, has nothing to tell. Least of all does it try to set going a 'soliloquy' in the Self to which it has appealed. 'Nothing' gets called *to* this Self, but it has been *summoned to* itself—that is, to its inmost potentiality-for-being" (p. 318). "The call comes *from* me and yet *from beyond me*" (p. 320). According to Heidegger, what happens in conscience is the call of care, summoning Dasein to its inmost potentiality of being. The uncanniness of this call has to be taken out of its self-forgetfulness. For this reason, what the call intimates is the possibility of authentic ability-to-be. And that is why, for Heidegger, anxiety is something in the nature of an enabling of this call, for it is in anxiety that we experience the isolation which is implied in authentic ability-to-be. The concept of guilt is here understood, not in a religious or moral sense but as "being-the-basis of a nullity (and this being-the-basis is itself null)" (p. 331).

The openness for the call of conscience is "willingness-to-have-a-conscience," a phenomenon which remains concealed for Everyman. This exposition of conscience culminates in a new definition of Dasein as *resoluteness (Entschlossenheit).** What does this mean? Willingness-to-have-a-conscience includes the experience of one's own nullity in anxiety, understanding as projecting oneself on one's inmost possibility, and speech. Resoluteness is a pre-eminent mode of *overtness (Erschlossenheit)*, the same concept in terms of which we attempted above to grasp the open-

---

* These words are dictionary equivalents. *Ent-schlossenheit*, however, also includes a suggestion of "dis-closedness," just as in optics "resolve" also has the sense of "rendering visible, opening up." It is this aspect of openness that Heidegger wants to emphasize, as opposed to the purely voluntaristic, surface meaning (Tr.).

ness of Dasein. The relation of resoluteness to truth is dealt with in the following section.

These fragmentary remarks were intended to enable us to move on to the question about the meaning of care, namely, about temporality as its real ground. The question Heidegger poses is *"What makes possible the totality of the articulated structural whole of care, in the unity of its articulation as we have unfolded it?"* (p. 371).

In anticipating the most extreme possibility (being toward death), Dasein simultaneously returns to its inmost has-been (*Gewesen*). It retains this has-been, it *is* its has-been. "Dasein can *be* its has-been only in so far as it is prospective [*zukünftig*]. The character of having-been arises, in a certain way, from the future" (p. 373). This is to turn upside-down the ordinary concept, according to which time moves forward, as it were, from the past to the present and then to the future. What is primary for Dasein is not the past, but the anticipation of what is not yet in being but which nevertheless appertains to me—as my death. Only because Dasein has the ability to anticipate, and is thus oriented to the future, is it possible for it to return to its has-been and so retain its has-been, not lose it. That, by the way, is also in its fashion the basic position of the entire literary work of Marcel Proust. It is from the perspective of the end, the foreboding of death, that the activity of writing is set in motion. And with this anticipation of the end, there goes hand in hand the retention of the has-been, the repetition of the has-been—in the act of writing. That is why this work has such a unique structure, with the development presented from the perspective of the end, as a return to the has-been. The experience of approaching death at the fancy dress ball of time is brought together with the childhood memory of the tinkling of the garden bell, which announces the visit of Swann, and the scene about the denied good-night kiss. Future, past and present have fused into a unity, the unity of time, which is the real protagonist in this work. At the very beginning of the work, we are already at its end, and the end throws us back to the beginning—to the comprehension and retention of the beginning, not just for the sake of retaining what has been but because the description of the has-been is at the same time the depiction of time.[10]

Through anticipation of the end (anticipatory resoluteness), Dasein acquires something like a *situation*, becomes situated. Dasein relates itself to entities as something to be concerned about, it lets them be encountered. ". . . actively letting that which is present in the environing world encounter us is possible only by means of a *present-ation* [*Gegenwärtigen*, making present] of that entity" (pp. 373–74). Such letting-encounter is part of resoluteness.

"Coming back to itself futurally, resoluteness brings itself into the situation by making present" (p. 374). This, however, is nothing else than the nature of temporality, as we may find it in the dimension of Dasein, as indeed it opens up and sustains the specific dimension of Dasein. Heidegger is thus led to say: *"Temporality reveals itself as the meaning of authentic care"* (p. 374). Having defined care as being-ahead-of-itself-in as being-beside, we can clearly see that being-ahead-of occurs in the temporalization of the future and being-beside is rendered possible through present-ation. Existentiality, facticity and forfeiture are gathered together in care. Existentiality involves projecting oneself, which is nothing else but the temporalization of the future. Facticity, or thrownness, was shown by us as the moment of being-already in care. "Only because care is based on the character of 'having-been', can Dasein exist as the thrown entity which it is" (p. 376).

Heidegger distinguishes between the has-been (*Gewesen-sein*) and the bygone (*Vergangen-sein*). The expression "bygone," or past, is applicable to entities of a type other than Dasein. The entity that exists—Dasein—is not bygone but has-been. "Has-been" carries a suggestion of still "be-ing." Facticity as a basic element in the constitution of Dasein is possible only because Dasein, in its temporal course, never leaves its has-been behind but is this has-been. The "ante" in "anticipation" and the "already" in "already-being-in" have reference to the temporal structure of care. What seemed at first to be the beginning of a purely descriptive procedure, but soon proved to be an inquiry back into the constitutive factors of the world, gains its proper justification in the interpretation of temporality as the basic structure of care. It should prove rewarding if a special attempt were for once made to lay open the exceedingly artful composition and inner structure of *Being and Time*, to show how, on the one hand, the work is based on close attention to the phenomena and how, on the other hand, the approach from the point of view of temporality determines the composition. We also see here the difference between Husserl and Heidegger in the style of their philosophizing. With Husserl, one gets the impression that he seeks to seize hold of the thing seen, pursuing ever-new adumbrations, as it were, and entirely taken up with description (comprehension). That is why the articulation has always to be inserted as an afterthought. It is, if anything, a summative exposition, resulting in the repetition of many analyses. With Heidegger, one gets the impression that the grasping of the articulation precedes the structure, and the exposition is carried out only after the articulation is grasped, so that no piece of analysis can be transferred to any other place. Hence, a correct understanding of *Being and Time*, too, must culminate in a grasp of the structure, and that means understanding it from the point of view of the end, from that of temporality.[11]

How do things stand in regard to the third component, forfeiture, or falling? Forfeiture is nothing but losing oneself in present-ation, in the sense of being-beside. It is, however, not possible without the future and the "it was."

"Temporality makes possible the unity of existence, facticity, and falling, and in this way constitutes primordially the totality of the structure of care" (p. 376).

Let us try to see how the existentialia—understanding, disposition, forfeiture and speech—are to be understood with special reference to temporality, or how authentic and inauthentic temporalization are different from each other. We have already pointed out that Heidegger's procedure is such that what has been analyzed previously is taken up again, though not in the sense of a mere repetition but rather from a new perspective, so that the resumed analysis advances our understanding of the structure. This does not by any means render the previous analysis superfluous, but only enables thinking to accomplish the task of providing a foundation for the facts.

How does the temporality of understanding exhibit itself? We saw that to understand is to project upon one's own possibilities of being, a disclosure of the ability-to-be. The various modes of "knowing" are based on such understanding. Projecting oneself upon one's possibilities, however, is nothing but a temporalization, a generating, of the future. "The future makes ontologically possible an entity which is in such a way that it exists understandingly in its potentiality-for-being" (p. 385). The possibility is not simply imagined, desired, hoped for or feared as a possibility. Rather, Dasein *is* such possibility, and only insofar as it is that does Dasein's future approach it. This manner of the temporalization, or being brought on, of the future is called by Heidegger "anticipation" (*Vorlaufen*, running ahead). The Dasein which temporalizes itself from its authentic future, that is, the future in which it attains to itself or realizes itself, is the *authentic* Dasein, and *anticipation* is the way it temporalizes the future.

How is inauthentic Dasein constituted? If care as a unitary structure is grounded in temporality, and if temporality includes the three ecstasies of future, past and present, then the future must be involved even in inauthentic Dasein. But in what manner? The analysis of everyday Dasein showed how Dasein is absorbed in concern, how it comprehends its own self in terms of concern and what the concern is about. "Dasein does not come towards itself primarily in its inmost non-relational potentiality-for-being, but *awaits this* concernfully *in terms of that which yields or denies the object of its concern*" (p. 386). The inauthentic future is an awaiting (*Gewärtigen*). Awaiting in turn makes possible the attitude of expecting, hoping, wishing.

The term which comprehends the authentic as well as inauthentic temporalization of the future is being-ahead-of-itself, the concept for grasping this existentiality.

Every temporalization, however, includes all three ecstasies. This has already been shown above, in so far as it was found that understanding, disposition and speech are equiprimordial. How can this be now demonstrated in the framework of the discovery of the temporal foundations of the existentialia?

Let us begin with the authentic temporalization of understanding, from the future. When Dasein anticipates, as in resoluteness, such anticipation involves "a present in accordance with which a resolution discloses the situation. In resoluteness, the present is not only brought back from distraction with the objects of one's closest concern, but it gets held in the future and in having-been. That *present* which is held in authentic temporality, and which thus is *authentic* itself, we call the '*moment of vision*' [*Augenblick*]" (p. 387).

The Moment is not a now-point in a temporal series. It is, rather, the manner in which Dasein is opened up to what meets it ·or, more precisely, to what it lets be encountered. That depends upon its own mode of being, upon its own ability to be itself.

The *inauthentic* temporalization of understanding has, in the ecstasy of the present, its corresponding present-ation. This means that the ability-to-be comprehends itself in terms of the object of concern that lies in front of it in the present. The authentic temporalization, on the contrary, temporalizes itself directly in terms of the future and does not forfeit itself to the object of concern.

How do things stand in respect to the third ecstasy? In authentic understanding, as we saw, Dasein temporalizes itself so that it keeps its character of having-been, and this in the very act of anticipating. The question discussed so often nowadays—how can one be, or become, identical with oneself?—is already anticipated here. "In anticipating, Dasein *brings* itself *again forth* into its inmost potentiality-for-being. If *being*-as-having-been is authentic, we call it '*repetition*' [*Wiederholung*]" (p. 388). When, on the other hand, the possibilities of Dasein are won only through its dealings with what it has to take care of, Dasein forgets what it already was, and along with it, what it can be. Heidegger expressly conceives of forgetting as a mode of the temporalization of the has-been, namely, as its inauthentic mode.

In literature we can easily find illustrations of how Dasein, while projecting its future, just does not want to see what it always was, how it denies its being as including the has-been and actually represses it. In this mode of being, Dasein shuts itself against itself, thus inevitably deluding itself about itself, and flies from itself (for example, Ibsen's *The Wild Duck*). This is unresoluteness, the opposite of the attitude which Heidegger conceives of as resolute-ness.*

The difficulty of a temporal interpretation of the existentialia also lies in this—that we have to keep in view the ecstasies in their totality and yet speak only about one of them at a time. Thus, in the temporal interpretation of understanding, in which the emphasis is on the ecstasy of the future, the present and past also come jointly into play.

Let us now try to delineate the temporal interpretation of *disposition*, or state-of-mind. We saw earlier that, according to Heidegger, attunement, or mood, discloses the thrownness of Dasein, the facticity of the *that* of this entity. But this means that moods are grounded in having-been (the past), as understanding is in the future.

". . . The existentially basic character of moods lies in *bringing* one *back to* something. This bringing-back does not first produce a having been; but in any state-of-mind some mode of having been is made manifest for existential analysis" (p. 390). This means that the character of having-been is not produced by a mood but that having-been can become manifest in moods because Dasein always was already, because it is its has-been.

By contrasting two moods, namely, fear and anxiety, Heidegger makes it evident that in fear, regarded as a kind of confusion, a self-forgetfulness manifests itself (inauthentic having-been), whereas in anxiety, what we see is just the futility of all concern, the impossibility of reaching oneself by way of the attitude of being concerned about something. In anxiety, Dasein comes back to itself—something in the nature of repetition occurs here. Dasein becomes aware of itself in its finitude. "Anxiety springs from the

* The two modes of temporalization, the authentic and the inauthentic, can be schematically contrasted as follows:

	Authentic temporalization	Inauthentic temporalization
Future	Anticipation	Awaiting
Present	Moment	Present-ation (making present)
Past (having-been-ness)	Repetition	Oblivion

future of resoluteness, while fear springs from the lost present, of which fear is fearfully apprehensive, so that it falls prey to it more than ever" (p. 395).

The temporality of forfeiture is elucidated by Heidegger in connection with curiosity. In curiosity there takes place a present-ation which, however, remains confined within the present because it is closed against the anticipation of its own possibilities. If the authentic present springs from the anticipation of the future and the retrieval of the has-been, curiosity has nothing to stand upon.

Otto Pöggeler has pointed out[12] that in the temporal analysis of these structural elements, speech has been substituted by the analysis of forfeiture. He attributed this to the fact that "Moment" has been given a minimal determination. As a matter of fact, in § 68 it is not speech but forfeiture that is discussed in the third place, and this is followed by a brief analysis of the temporal structure of speech. Thus, the triad of the ecstasies of time is applied here to a quaternity of phenomena, which presents a certain break in the arrangement. However, we should not overlook the fact that the temporal groundwork refers to the basic modalities of the existence, facticity and forfeiture of Dasein, and to that extent the triad of ecstasies does fulfill its function of providing a foundation. In his analysis of speech, Heidegger shows how in it a preferred significance attaches to present-ation, insofar as speech is mostly about what is encountered in the environing world. This does not, however, exhaust its function, as the example of art shows.

It should be kept in mind, in respect to the structure, that in every temporalization all three ecstasies are involved, though in understanding it is the future, in disposition, the past, and in forfeiture and speech, the present, that have priority. The aim was to exhibit the temporal structure of care and that is what these analyses have accomplished. We cannot here go into the renewed interpretation of being-in-the-world (§ 69), important as it is, or into § 70—"The temporality of the spatiality that is characteristic of Dasein"—nor can we deal with the connection between temporality and historicity.

As already mentioned, the whole questioning was to be turned round in the third division of the first part: Time and Being. This division was not published.

THE PROBLEM OF TRUTH (ON § 44)

The exposition of care as the being of Dasein culminates in the inquiry into the connection between Being and truth. This connection is not arbitrarily posited, nor is it an invention. Heidegger shows, on the contrary, how philosophical thought circles round the connection between Being and truth from its very beginning. This is particularly evident in Parmenides, but also in Aristotle, who defines philosophy as ἐπιστήμη τῆς ἀληθείας and at the same time as the *episteme* which considers beings as beings, thus, in respect of their being. Must not an investigation which calls itself, and conceives itself as, fundamental-ontological, inquire into this connection? Indeed, it must. This means that the connection between Dasein and truth must be made thematic, so that we may see "why Being necessarily goes together with truth and *vice versa*" (p. 256).

The investigation is arranged in three steps: (1) the traditional concept of truth and its ontological foundations; (2) the primordial phenomenon of truth and an account of the derivative character of the traditional concept; and (3) the mode of being of truth and the presupposition of truth.

The direction of the inquiry is characteristic of Heidegger. Starting from the common understanding of truth—hardened and appearing, because of this hardening, as if it were definitive—the inquiry moves backward to the primordial phenomenon, as it is prior to the hardening by which it has been covered up. The usual concept of truth takes a statement as the real locus of truth and sees its essence itself as lying in the correspondence of a judgment with its object. In doing so, it appeals to the authority of Aristotle, who is supposed to have assigned this locus to truth and to have defined truth in terms of correspondence.

The statement of Aristotle that the "experiences" of the soul are in the likeness of things, which is not at all meant to be taken as a definition of the essential nature of truth (*De interpretatione* I, 16a, 6), led in the Middle Ages to the definition of *veritas* as *adaequatio intellectus et rei*, a definition which has maintained its hold beyond Kant. Heidegger asks: What is here the meaning of correspondence—*adaequatio*—ὁμοίωσις? Taken formally, it is a relation of something to something (p. 258), though not every relation is one of correspondence. The peculiar characteristic of this relation has therefore to be explained.

Since they are in no way similar, in what respect can the intellect and the thing correspond (compare "On the Essence of Truth," in *Existence and Being*, p. 296)? The intellect must grasp the thing as it is. How can it do this without itself becoming the thing?

In a judgment we can distinguish between the act of judging and that which is judged. The act of judging is a real psychical process; what is judged is an ideal content. We do not at all need to know what psychical processes are occurring in someone who is judging. The matter has now become even more complicated. On the one side we have the real act of judging, and on the other, the ideal content thought about in the act. This content, however, is in turn supposed to refer to something real, when our judgment is about a concrete state of affairs. "Does not the actuality of knowing and judging get broken asunder into two ways of Being—two 'levels' which can never be pieced together in such a manner as to reach the kind of being that belongs to knowing?" (p. 259).

"When does truth become phenomenally explicit in knowledge itself? It does so when such knowing demonstrates itself *as true*" (p. 260). But when is this the case?—that is, after all, the question. "Thus in the phenomenal context of demonstration [*Ausweisung*], the relationship of agreement must become visible" (p. 260). How are we to conceive of such proof? Heidegger takes a quite simple example. I make a statement about a picture hanging on the wall, without seeing the picture itself. Then I turn round and look at it, to see whether the statement is right. The statement is: The picture on the wall is hanging askew. In what does the verification of the statement, or its falsification, consist? It should be noted in the first place that when I make the statement, I am not concerned with any psychical phenomenon or process of representation; I am, rather, concerned with the thing itself. We need not at present go into the question as to what different possibilities there are of being with the thing itself. "Asserting is a way of being towards the thing itself that is" (p. 260). In this case the proof is in the perception. What happens when a statement is verified? An entity becomes accessible in its being: it is discovered.

The knowing which is involved in stating something is a relationship with entities which discovers them, lays them bare. The chief stress here is on such discovering, or laying open, not on any possible conformity of psychical processes to ideal contents, which are then assigned to something real. The purport of a statement is to let us see that about which something is stated, the particular entity, in other words. To be true is to-be-discovering (*Entdeckendsein*). In order that Dasein should be in a position to achieve such a thing, it must be constituted as being-in-the-world. It is precisely this that the second step goes on to consider.

In connection with this interpretation of truth as to-be-discovering, Heidegger refers to the beginning of philosophy. In the first fragment of Heraclitus, *logos* is declared to be that which tells us how it is with things—the foolish forget it; it sinks back into hiddenness for them.

In translating *aletheia* as unhiddenness (*Unverborgenheit*), Heidegger's aim is by no means to provide merely a more literal translation but, on the contrary, to bring into view the experience which is associated with this phenomenon. This is the really phenomenological trend, one which he himself finds already present in Aristotle. When we use the word "truth," we think we know what *aletheia* means; but basically we only substitute the Greek word with another, in order to spare ourselves the trouble of pondering what is truly happening here. In Aristotle, *logos* as ἀπόφανσις is an ἀληθεύειν in the sense of ἀποφαίνεσθαι, that is to say, a letting-be-seen of the entities that are brought from hiddenness into unhiddenness. What is thus disclosed are the things themselves, "*entities in the 'how' of their discoveredness*" (p. 262).

We shall have to consider carefully, as we progress, the details of how unhiddenness is thought and experienced. In this matter, it should be noted, Heidegger's thinking changed (compare *On Time and Being,* p. 70). Here, our concern is to find out the connection between *aletheia* and Dasein. In this context, ἀληθεύειν, or being true, is regarded as a mode of being of Dasein (p. 263), namely, one in which Dasein acts in a "discovering"— we might also say uncovering, laying open—manner, lets something become accessible without cover. Thus, what is true in a primary sense is this mode of acting itself, and, only secondarily, that which becomes accessible as a result of acting in this way, the entity which is in each case discovered. That is why Heidegger requires us to regard that as the primordial phenomenon of truth which renders possible this to-be-discovering itself. That is, as shown earlier, the overtness of Dasein, in other words, its being-in-the-world, as constituted by disposition, understanding and speech, in the sense of care. Care, as thus understood, is also that which takes up into a unity the three modes of temporalization of future, past (has-been-ness) and present.

The expression *"Dasein is 'in the truth' "* (p. 263) does not mean, of course, that Dasein is in possession of all truth, which would be absurd. It means that because of its overtness, which includes its to-be-discovering, Dasein is in a position to "disclose." Dasein can be discovering—thus making entities available to itself, inquiring about them, explaining them, forming them and so on— only because it is capable of standing in some relation to itself, in the sense of being alert and open.

One might object that this is nothing but the classic modern definition: Consciousness is self-consciousness. Actually, however, this is something different, for the concept of Dasein is not just another term for the subject. Dasein is conceived, rather, as being-in-the-world. The starting point is never the isolated subject, from which then the transition to the transcendent has to be made. Rather, from the very beginning, being-in-the-world is comprehended as a fundamental structure and it is shown what this fundamental structure includes, which are the existentialia, and how they are grounded in the temporalization of Dasein. These are genuine insights, formerly nonexistent.

Being-in-the-world means for Heidegger that the overtness of Dasein involves the articulated structure of care as a whole, including the factor of projection (the temporalization of the future) —Dasein projects itself on its possibilities, opening up its world for itself—and the factor of thrownness—Dasein finds itself always in a particular world, and this presupposes the temporalization of the has-been.

We should remember here that in projecting, Dasein may comprehend itself on the basis of its very own possibilities (authenticity). When this happens, we have the *"truth of existence"* (p. 264). Or, it may understand itself in terms of the world, to which it has ever already forfeited itself (inauthenticity). Dasein is then in untruth. As we have seen earlier, so far as Dasein exists, in the first place and mostly, in the mode of inauthenticity, it is (as forfeited or fallen) in untruth. Dasein is thus in truth and in untruth.

That which has been discovered by Dasein must be expressly guarded, in respect to this discoveredness, so that it may not lapse into dissimulation, or illusion; discoveredness must be wrested from illusion.

In the *alpha* of *aletheia* Heidegger sees an *alpha-privativum*. "Entities are snatched out of hiddenness. Every factual discoveredness is always, as it were, a robbery" (p. 265). When Parmenides places the goddess of truth in front of two paths, those of discovering and concealing, this marks for Heidegger an early insight into the fact that man stands in truth as well as in untruth.

The upshot of these remarks is, first, that the primordial truth is the overtness of Dasein, and this includes not only the openness of Dasein to itself but also the discoveredness of entities from its world; secondly, that Dasein is equioriginally in truth and in untruth.

Having seen earlier that Dasein is distinguished from all other beings by its understanding of Being, we may now add that this understanding of Being is itself possible because Dasein exists in the mode of being overt. Existing in this fashion, it stands out against ready-to-hand entities (articles of use) and present-at-hand entities (those which are just there by themselves), which exhibit other modes of being.

The discussion of truth is again taken up (to make just a brief reference to this) in § 61 and § 62, in connection with the temporal interpretation of care and the account of Dasein as "existentially authentic ability-to-be-whole" (p. 352).

"Resoluteness becomes authentically what it can be, as *comprehendingly being towards* [*in relation to*], *that is, as anticipating death*" (p. 353). In resoluteness, Dasein is pulled back to its own inmost selfhood. But if truth is grounded in Dasein, if being true— that is, the primary openness—is a mode of being-there (Dasein), then we must say, consequentially, that resoluteness is "the primordial *truth* of existence" (p. 355). While existing in the mode of resoluteness, Dasein is primordially in truth.

The problem of truth is given its first published treatment in *Being and Time*. In it, the traditional concept of truth—truth as correspondence—is traced back to the constitution of Dasein as to-be-discovering and open to itself. That Dasein is in truth does not mean that truths are planted in it by some mysterious power, but that by virtue of being-in-the-world, it is always already open for all that is part of its world. The new approach to the understanding of man as Dasein leads to the new interpretation and exposition of truth. It is no accident that in the process Heidegger goes back to the earliest thinkers and comes to grips with the founders of metaphysics. For, it is in these first thinkers that he finds the thoughts which anticipate those that appeared later and which come down to us as a task for our own thinking.

The being of man as Dasein is thematically treated in *Being and Time*. But this topic was intended as only a preparation for the development of the question about the meaning of Being, which was held back. If the analysis developed here is in the nature of a preparation for the proper subject of the inquiry, then it may be assumed that the comments on truth in § 49 also do not represent the last word on this question but rather a beginning for what is yet to be said. Where do we find the continuation of this inquiry into truth? In the lecture "On the Essence of Truth." It should be examined with a view to finding out how far it takes us beyond § 44 of *Being and Time*. When we do so, it will only strengthen the impression, which we already had from *Being and Time*, that for pursuing the inquiry in the direction opened up here, no help was to be expected from transcendental philosophy, nor from German Idealism or phenomenology.

16. The Heidegger family, 1924

17. Aristotle (The Louvre, Paris)

18. Plato (The Vatican, Rome)

19. Immanuel Kant
(painting by Gottlieb Doeppler, 1791)

20. The University of Marburg

21. Hannah Arendt

22. Shoes (painting by Vincent van Gogh)

23. The University of Freiburg

24. The house (middle foreground) where *Being and Time* was written

25. View from Heidegger's study

28. Georg Wilhelm Friedrich Hegel
(painting by Jack Schlesinger)

27. Friedrich Hölderlin (pastel by F. K. Heimer,
private collection, Stuttgart)

29. Temple of Aphaia
on the island of Aegina (500–490 B.C.)

(5

The Problem of Truth in "On the Essence of Truth" (1930)

Let us try to understand the construction of this lecture.[13] It is one of Heidegger's writings, the composition of which is particularly rigorous.

In the introduction, the subject of the inquiry is outlined. It is the *essence* of truth that is to be examined, not the various kinds of truth with which we are familiar, ranging from the practical, political and scientific to the artistic and religious. Obviously, as we are led by this introduction into the main problem, we notice something of the plurality of voices in the composition. A second voice emerges clearly, the voice of common sense, for which a problem of essence such as this is simply meaningless. It confronts the problem of essence with its own question, the search for "the actual truth which can give us a standard and a yardstick" (p. 282).* This is not just a rhetorical contrast, but situates us right at the beginning within the antagonism existing between the quest of philosophy and the demands of common sense. The argument between common sense and philosophy is indeed a hopeless affair, for common sense can only regard philosophy as a useless enterprise. And it is critical of art as well, for art is equally useless, unless we take it as a means of relaxing after the exertions of the day. From philosophy, not even this can be expected; it demands from us, rather, the utmost concentration.

* Unless otherwise mentioned, page references in this chapter are to the translation of this eassay by R. F. C. Hull and Alan Crick, in *Existence and Being* (Chicago: Regnery, 1949), which has been modified in some cases.

On the other hand, from the side of philosophy, it cannot be denied that common sense is indispensable for our daily life. Moreover, the beliefs of common sense have greater influence than we are willing to acknowledge. We are ourselves, too, under the domination of these beliefs when we assume that it is the variety of truths mentioned above that imparts security and stability to our existence (p. 293).

The dispute between philosophy and common sense has its roots in the very origins of philosophy, and it can be followed from Plato to Hegel and Nietzsche, not to mention Heidegger. Whether contemporary positivism is not just the current form of common sense is also a question worth examining.

The conflict within which the introduction has situated us can in no way be resolved by fiat or explained away. It confronts us with the question of what we mean by truth when, time and again, we speak of truth. For even common sense employs this word. It does not at all deny the possibility of truth, even though the demand for efficacy and utility is always present in the background.

How is the inquiry carried out? We can distinguish two steps. The first step starts out from the common concept of truth, namely, truth in the sense of correspondence, and inquires into what is presupposed in this concept of truth, into what must therefore be laid bare, so that we may really be able to grasp this concept. This regressive inquiry is an inquiry into that which renders this concept possible. It comprises the first three sections of the text. (The further subdivisions will be explained presently.) The outcome to this backtracking inquiry is thought through in a second step (it covers §§ 4 to 7 of the text), as a result of which the problem of truth emerges in a new light. The second step continues the process of questioning, but now on the basis which has been prepared by the first step. Here it becomes evident how the nature of man himself must be thought anew in consequence of this questioning. We see how in this second step of thought the inquirer himself is changed. The conclusions of his thinking are not just any results, however important they may be, of which cognizance is simply to be taken. Rather, these conclusions touch, enter into, the being of the inquirer himself. We are provided with an exposition of the nature of Dasein as it must be understood in terms of the nature of truth. The exposition leads to a new determination of the nature of philosophy itself, which concludes the text (compare Chapter 10). The conclusion, however, does not constitute the end, in the sense of reaching the goal, but rather points forward to a beginning which remains to be made afresh. Heidegger goes into this expressly in his concluding remarks, but that is excluded from our purview here.

After this necessarily superficial account of the construction of the essay, let us try now to give an outline of the course of thought in terms of its content.

The common concept of truth takes correspondence as its basic feature. That which makes a true thing a thing that is true is in every case correspondence. But what does correspondence mean here? What corresponds with what? While discussing § 44 of *Being and Time*, we saw how Heidegger puts into question this concept of truth, how he contrasts truth as correspondence with truth as unhiddenness and the manner in which he explains how truth can be equated with correspondence and judgment taken to be the locus of truth. Here he proceeds in a different way, without rejecting, however, the conclusions arrived at in *Being and Time*.

It is not merely a judgment, of course, that we call true. Ordinarily, we also speak of a state of affairs as true, and this may apply either to human beings—their state (feelings) or their behavior (say, friendship)—or to things (for example, money). The first explanation seeks to identify the true with the real, but then the money which has turned out to be counterfeit is also something real, otherwise we could never be exposed to the risk of being deceived by it. When here, in the thing, we thus equate true and real, this means that we have a certain concept of the thing, and when the thing corresponds with this concept, we say that it is true—that is to say, it is right, it is as it should be.

The next consideration pertains to statements, which we usually call true or false. "A statement is true when what it means and says agrees with the thing of which it speaks" (p. 295). Thus, in the first case it is the thing that is right; now it is the proposition that is right. Hence, being right or corresponding (*Stimmen*) is itself capable of being understood in two different ways: "firstly, the correspondence of a thing with the idea of it as conceived in advance, and secondly, the correspondence of that which is intended by the statement with the thing itself" (p. 295).

The traditional definition of truth, *veritas est adaequatio rei et intellectus*, already contains this capability of being interpreted in two ways. For the *adaequatio* may mean "the approximation of thing [object] to perception" (p. 295) or the approximation of perception to thing. It is true that that definition is generally understood in the sense of propositional truth (the approximation of a statement to what it is about). But then, for propositional truth to be possible at all, it is necessary that we have a definite conception of the thing, so that the propositional truth may remain related to objective truth (*Sachwahrheit*). In the case of both "truths," truth is conceived as conforming-with (thing and preconception; sentence and thing) and it is equated with rightness or correctness. Further, it should not be overlooked that in the medieval interpretation each version of conformity contains two meanings of *intellectus*. The conformity of a thing with the intellect has reference to the divine intellect and not to the intellect of man, as we first took to be the case when we started out, and as it is regarded also in the transcendental mode of inquiry in Kant, according to which we can acquire *a priori* knowledge only when we have realized that it is objects that must conform to knowledge. As created by God, things are created in accordance with His ideas and thus they necessarily conform to His ideas. The human intellect, too, is created by God and must also, therefore, satisfy the divine idea.

"The *intellectus humanus* is likewise an *ens creatum*. It must, as a faculty conferred by God on man, satisfy His idea. But the intellect only conforms to the idea in that it effects in its propositions that approximation of thought to thing, which, in its turn, must also conform to the idea. The possibility of human knowledge being true (granted that all that 'is' is created) has its basis in the fact that thing and proposition are to an equal extent in conformity with the idea and thus find themselves conforming to one another in the unity of the divine creative plan" (p. 296). We have here a justification for agreement, in the sense of propositional truth, provided by the coordination of man and thing in accordance with the plan of creation. "*Veritas* always means in its essence: *convenientia*, the accord of 'what-is' itself, as created, with the Creator, an accordance with the destiny of the creative order" (pp. 296–97).

It is not at all Heidegger's concern to justify this interpretation; it is rather to show how it was interpreted in the Middle Ages and thus to draw our attention to the curious fact that this interpretation of truth as correspondence is retained even when the medieval position is abandoned. The rationality of the world, world-reason (*Weltvernunft*), now takes the place of God as Creator. "The creative order as conceived by theology is supplanted by the possibility of planning everything with the aid of worldly reason, which is a law unto itself and can claim that its workings . . . are immediately intelligible" (p. 297). Even where this position is abandoned, the interpretation of truth as the correctness of correspondence survives, acquiring a quasi-absolute validity, and it is forgotten how this interpretation was originally justified.

Having thus gained general acceptance, this concept of truth appears self-evident, that is, not in need of any further substantiation. It is this self-evidence that Heidegger attacks. It has become questionable to him, as much so as the view that there must also be something which is the opposite of truth, namely, untruth.

Cannot this obvious concept of truth as correspondence be saved by reducing objective truth to propositional truth? And may we not even appeal to the authority of Aristotle for this purpose and to the view that "truth is the *likeness* or *agreement* [*Übereinstimmung*] (ὁμοίωσις) of a statement (λόγος) to or with a given thing (πρᾶγμα)" (p. 298)? We remember, of course, the remarks in *Being and Time* showing how the appeal to Aristotle does not touch the core of the matter.

What does correspondence really mean? This is the next question that has to be clarified. It constitutes the second stage in the first step of the argument. First of all, we may speak of correspondence between two things when, in fact, they have the same appearance. In that case, they correspond in respect to their appearance. They certainly do not become *one;* each remains what it is—but what is common to them is just the sameness of appearance. In the context of the problem of truth, however, another kind of correspondence is meant, namely, the correspondence between a statement and a thing or matter.

But then, how can two such disparate "things" as sentence and matter correspond? Let us take, as an example, the sentence: This house is big. The house is built of stone, the sentence is not material at all. We can live in a house, we can rent it or sell it, none of which applies to the sentence. To what extent can we then speak of correspondence? How can the sentence, so unlike a house, correspond to the house when it says something about the house? Naturally, this cannot imply that the sentence turns into a house. On the contrary, it must remain a sentence if it is to say anything. Obviously, the approximation of a sentence (statement) to some matter (thing) means here a special kind of relation. But of what kind?

Heidegger calls it a re-presentative (*vor-stellende*) relation, in which the statement is keyed to the thing and says something about how it is or what it is like in any particular respect. Representing is not meant here in a psychological sense, as a particular act of consciousness, having such and such a structure. Heidegger thinks of representing (*Vor-stellen*) as *"letting something take up a position opposite to us, as an object"* (p. 300). How does anything like this take place? Or, in other words, what happens in representing understood in this sense? "The thing so opposed must, such being its position, come across the open towards us and at the same time stand fast in itself as the thing and manifest itself as something constant" (p. 300).

So far, Heidegger has given the impression that all he is doing is just describing some state of affairs. But now we see unmistakably that every kind of pure description has long been abandoned. We are in the presence of an interpretive procedure which seeks to clarify for us the perplexing phenomenon of our encountering and comprehending entities. In what manner is it carried out here? Certainly not in Husserl's manner of explaining the transcendence of consciousness by means of intentionality. Everything connected with the theory of consciousness is ruled out. In order that the person who states something may represent anything as an ob-ject (*Gegen-stand*), the thing must show itself, it must enter into a realm which Heidegger calls "the realm of the open," or of the unhidden. What leads to the emergence of a realm of openness is not discussed here, but a possible misconception is removed—the misconception that this realm is created by the representing subject, that how an entity is to show itself is thus determined by the representing agent through the act of representing. This possibility is rejected by Heidegger. The domain of the open is not created by the representing subject; on the contrary, the latter has to place himself also in this sphere. A relationship between the representer and the represented thus comes about, which Heidegger conceives of as "relating" (*Verhalten*, having a relation, comportment, attitude to) which "is distinguished by the fact that, obtaining in the open, it always holds itself in a relation to something manifest *as such*" (p. 301).

As we have it in the unpublished first version of the lecture, "All 'relating' as such contains, as part of what it bestows, the inner mandate to get in tune with that to which the 'relating' holds itself in relation and how it holds itself toward it. The becoming attuned of this holding-in-relation, moreover, is an opening itself to that toward which it holds itself, and, together with it, a being open to that of the 'relating' itself." And further, "the 'relating' is 'being in tune with' that makes something manifest" (unpublished lecture).

In the printed version, Heidegger goes on to point out that what becomes manifest in the "relating" was conceived by the Greeks as that which is present (*das Anwesende*). This indicates the dimension which is to be surveyed in this lecture, namely, European metaphysics.

How is this "relating" to be thought about more fully? Heidegger calls it the relationship or attitude of overtness, for what concerns him is the fact that in "relating," entities may be encountered, which is possible because the "relating" is a standing-in-the-open and is at the same time itself open for what is encountered there, that which is manifest. Evidently, all religious and theological suggestions must be excluded from this concept. What is manifest is simply that which is present, which is available in its presence, though this does not mean necessarily that this presence as such becomes thematic. The manifest is that which shows itself to Dasein. We should not, of course, think of this as though entities come marching on the stage and all we have to do is to hold fast to or notice this fact. The manner of standing-in-the-open, or of overtness, varies according to the mode of "relating." "Relating" is by no means a passive reception. On the contrary, it is in "relating" and through it that the overtness is sustained. "All working and carrying out of tasks, all transaction and calculation, sustains itself in the open, an overt region within which what-is can expressly place itself, *as* and *how* it is *what* it is, and thus become capable of expression" (p. 301). We need not here take up the question as to how in this placing itself by an entity the latter can become present in various ways, depending on the mode of our access to it, or, more precisely, on the character of the openness in which it manifests itself. The transformation of this openness concerns precisely the historical dimension proper.

A statement about a manifest, self-exhibiting entity hits the mark when the statement submits itself to such an entity or plays up to it. The statement then states how it is with the entity which shows itself. The statement conforms to, is governed by (*sich richtet nach*), the entity in this manner, when it takes its directive for what it says from the entity itself. "Directing itself in this way the statement is right (true). And what is thus stated is rightness (truth)" (p. 301).

A statement is not an all-powerful instrument by means of which we take possession, so to speak, of a thing. On the contrary, a statement depends upon our overtness, since what-is can show itself only by reason of the overtness of Dasein and since we can receive from the entity alone the directive to say something about it which applies to it, or, according to an earlier formulation, since we are capable of playing up to it. The criterion for the statement must originate with the entities themselves. We may not simply fall upon what-is and intrude, force something, upon it. When anything of this sort occurs, we only do violence to what-is, which is not, indeed, beyond the realm of possibility.

Why has this matter been presented in such detail? Because it is the pivot for unfolding the problematics of truth in a manner that goes beyond the traditional understanding, which has held its ground up to the present. For, if every statement depends upon the possibility of the overtness of Dasein, upon the overtness of its attitude, then this overt comportment "must have a more original claim to be regarded as the essence of truth" (p. 302).

With this we come to the third development within the first step of the inquiry, namely, to the question about "The Basis of the Inner Possibility of Rightness" (p. 303). The situation in which we find ourselves is made clear by the following questions: "Whence does the representative statement receive its command to be governed by the object and thus to agree with it according to rightness? Why does this agreement at the same time determine [bestimmen] the nature of truth? How, in fact, can there be such a thing at all as the laying down of a pre-established criterion, or a directive enjoining such an accord?" Heidegger answers: "only because this pre-giving has already freed itself [sich freigegeben hat] and become open to a manifestation operating in this openness—a manifestation which is binding on all representation whatsoever" (p. 303). In this step of the inquiry, therefore, we must lay bare the ground of the possibility of conforming to what-is. Releasing oneself for the entity that is manifest is "being free towards what is manifest in the open" (p. 303). With this, the consideration of the nature of truth is given an unexpected turn, for now it becomes evident that "the essence of truth is freedom" (p. 303).

Until now, perhaps, we may have been under the impression that Heidegger seeks only to justify the traditional concept of truth, as it were, in the manner of transcendental philosophy. That this is not the case should now be beyond doubt. For, the reduction of the essence of truth to freedom is not only something unwonted but actually a provocation—unless, of course, we try to recast and render innocuous this thesis of Heidegger's by maintaining that, obviously, some sort of freedom is implied in making a statement, in the sense that we may make it or refrain from doing so. This misconception is at once rejected in the text. ". . . Our proposition in no way implies that the making of the statement, or the communication and adoption of it, involves voluntary action. The proposition says: Freedom is the *essence of truth itself*" (p. 303). It is, hence, that on which truth is based, by which it is rendered possible. But the traditional concept of truth by no means contains this idea.

We need not go into the various objections against this thesis, for they all start out from a naïve understanding of what freedom is. Its guiding idea is that "freedom is a property of man" (p. 304). If this unexamined concept no longer has any validity and indeed has no place in the realm in which Heidegger's questioning-back moves, then the nature of freedom must expressly be drawn into this inquiry. With that, the traditional domain of the problem of truth is unequivocally abandoned. This question now resides in a domain which is unfamiliar and for that reason seems strange.

The second step of thinking in the essay begins with this fresh approach in the inquiry, by way of a discussion of freedom as the foundation of truth. In this step it is not only the nature of truth that is inquired into but also the nature of man himself. The direction of the inquiry is indicated at the very beginning of § 4: ". . . freedom is the basis of the inner possibility of rightness only because it receives its own essence from the more primordial essence of the uniquely essential truth" (p. 305). This examination of the nature of freedom has not brought us to the conclusion of the inquiry, however. We must take yet another step backward in order to see what is the basis of freedom itself and what renders it possible. To move forward in this direction, it is necessary to discuss first how freedom is to be conceived here.

So far, freedom has been exhibited as man's overtness (*Offenständigkeit*). Standing in the realm of the open, he is able to subject himself to what is manifest and shows itself in it, and to bind or commit himself to it. With this binding, there takes place a letting-be (*Sein-lassen*). Again, this is an expression which can easily be misunderstood, because in common usage it (*Lassen*, letting) carries the sense of disregarding, of omission and indifference. For Heidegger, "letting-be" means "to consent or yield [*sich einlassen*] to what-is" (p. 306). Letting-be is not just any activity of man, but is that by virtue of which he becomes *Da-sein*, an entity that is defined by its relationship to the open. "Letting-be

. . . means participating in the open and its openness, within which every entity enters and stands" (p. 306).

The Greeks thought of the open as the unconcealed (τὰ ἀληθέα). Because Dasein holds itself in the open, it is able to inquire into what shows itself as manifest in it, to let that itself speak out, as it were, and this in turn means, for the act of representing, to let the criterion be provided by the entities themselves. The revealing (to Dasein) of entities and binding itself (by Dasein) to entities are not two distinct processes but one and the same. Dasein exposes itself to what-is— it is *ek-sistent*, or ex-sistent. Existing here does not mean seizing hold of certain possibilities of being in the sense of realizing one's self but this peculiar letting-be, which precedes all our comportment and ways of relating ourselves. Freedom itself is ex-sistent: "an 'exposition' into the revealed nature [*Entborgenheit*, unveiledness] of what-is" (p. 307).

Heidegger's thinking quite explicitly focuses on this uncovered-ness. To grasp it and give it utterance, to analyze it, to bring it before our discerning eye, this is the task with which he wrestles. Uncoveredness becomes, as it were, the foundation of man, so that he can be understood only on the basis of this underlying principle. This uncoveredness or disclosedness is preserved by man in "ex-sistent participation or letting-oneself-into" (p. 307). Once we see that this is the basic principle in man as Heidegger views him, it becomes clear why, from *Being and Time* onward, he speaks of Dasein instead of man. For, man is man only by virtue of being in the open, standing in the open and letting be what is manifested. Unconcealment is experienced at the moment "when the first thinker inquiringly confronts the unhiddeness of what-is [entities] with the question of what entities are" (p. 308). According to Heidegger, this is a great moment because it also signifies the beginning of historical existence, of the history of the West. It is the moment when the Greeks experienced what is termed φύσις. Simultaneous with the beginning of history, there occurs the experience of Nature, which is itself without history. History happens as the manner of man's overtness from time to time. What is ordinarily called history, the period of conquerors, wars and the like, is something only secondary compared with the openness in which mankind (a people) stands at any particular time—the openness which it guards and which is the basis of its entire relationship to what-is.

Heidegger concludes from this that "man does not 'possess' freedom as a property; it is the contrary that is true: freedom, or ex-sistent, revelatory *Da-sein*, possesses man and, moreover, in so original a manner that it alone confers upon him that relationship with what-is-in-totality which is the basis and distinctive characteristic of his history" (pp. 308–9).

In the letting-be of entities truth happens. Truth is "the revelation of what-is, a revelation through which an openness occurs" (p. 309). Our immediate tendency is to take this in the sense that this openness is an achievement of man, by reason of which he has control over entities. This is not what is said here; rather, every activity or relationship has its basis in the openness in which man is placed. Rightness as explained previously, in the sense of approximation to an entity that has become representable, is possible only when Dasein is conceived as an entity that is overt.

Truth is here consistently thought of as the ground which renders possible this overtness; at the same time, reference is made to the fact that man stands out—ex-sists—in truth as so understood, in truth regarded as unhiddenness, so that his fundamental decisions are based on the way beings in their totality are comprehended. This is truth in the sense of *aletheia*.

The difficulties which we encounter here do not lie in the opacity of Heidegger's language but in the circumstance that Heidegger is pushing forward into a domain with which we are unfamiliar. What here is unfamiliar cannot be rendered accessible with the use of familiar words, nor with entirely unfamiliar ones. Heidegger attempts here to lay open a basic experience underlying the fact that man's way of being is historical (*Geschichtlich*). The horizon of history is the horizon of possible interpretations of what-is as such, in which the particular interpretation given at any time, the prevailing epochal understanding of beings, forms the basis of the entire behavior of Dasein. But we cannot say why just the interpretation of beings as *physis* is the first and why this is later followed by certain other interpretations. What, however, we must inquire into are the implications of each interpretation, implications which were not noticed as such at first.

The further we advance in our reading of the lecture on truth, the more difficult becomes the state of affairs. It is an advance into perfectly new territory. When an interpretation leads to some simplification, we immediately tend to accept it. When, on the contrary, an interpretation demands that we grapple with an unusual difficulty, we reject it. This seems to be true altogether of the present-day attitude to Heidegger. He is rejected or ignored at the point when he demands from us the effort of thinking—without, in addition, giving us any assurance whatever that he is in possession of absolute truth. He himself, it is true, is not concerned about such rejection or agreement, but is concerned, rather, with paving a new way of thinking, and doing this, too, with ever-new approaches and fresh starts. It will be a long time before these starts are understood; today that is not yet the case.

We started out from the point that, in the act of representing, we can let an entity itself lay its claim upon us and become representable. Man establishes, in this way, a bond with beings—because truth in its essence is freedom. But it is just this characteristic which makes it also possible for man not to let what-is be, as it is, but cover and misrepresent it. That is the dominion of illusion— the sway of the disessence of truth. But if freedom is not an attribute of man, if he exists rather "as the property" of freedom itself, then untruth also should not be attributed simply to man as a kind of failure. "If the essence of truth is not fully displayed in the rightness of a statement, then neither can untruth be equated with the wrongness of judgment" (p. 310).

The inquiry into the connection between truth and untruth is to be pursued further; that is the second stage within the second step of thought. First, we are led into a deeper probing of the meaning of mood or attunement, which is familiar to us as an existential from *Being and Time*. Whereas attunement was analyzed there in connection with the movement of thrownness and also as the primordial mode of the disclosure of world, here it is taken as a manifestation of the primordial openness, which corresponds with our relationship to what-is in its totality and is based on it. Being attuned means "an ex-sistent exposition into what-is-in-totality" (p. 311).

This does not invalidate the previous analysis of attunement. But Heidegger does not rest content with that. He moves on in search of a fundamental attunement and finds it in the primordial relationship with beings in their totality. "Man's behavior is attuned to the manifest character of what-is-in-totality" (p. 312). Usually, we cling to the particular entity that is at the moment manifest; what is as a whole is just that which does not become thematic. This means that that to which we are attuned actually conceals itself. In the letting-be itself we have simultaneously a yielding to what-is at the moment and the concealment of what-is as a whole. "In the ex-sistent freedom of Dasein, there takes place a hiding of what-is in totality, is concealedness [Verborgenheit]" (p. 312).

How, if at all, does concealedness become accessible to thinking? "From the point of view of truth conceived as revealedness . . . hiddenness is un-revealedness [Un-entborgenheit] and thus the untruth proper which is intrinsic to the nature of truth" (p. 313). Disclosure of any kind can take place only on the basis of concealedness. While letting an entity be, Dasein relates itself to this hiddenness, but only in such a way that the hiddenness itself remains concealed from it. This, according to Heidegger, is the "mystery."

"Letting things as a whole be—a process which reveals and conceals at the same time—brings it about that concealment appears as the initial thing concealed" (p. 313). This means that a thinking which seeks to reach out to beings in their totality encounters hiddenness and experiences it as the original nature of truth, which means, as untruth. It is true that concealedness is the basis of all disclosure, but ordinarily, which means traditionally, we are so thoroughly captivated by the thing that is revealed that concealedness itself—the mystery—lapses into oblivion. This happens also in metaphysics, which does indeed reach out in its thinking to what-is as such, giving rise in the course of its development to various meanings of what-is, but which does not make concealedness itself thematic.

Oblivion of the mystery does not in any way make it lose its potency. Rather, the backlash of this forgetting expresses itself in the fact that man clings to what is "practicable" and at the same time poses as the absolute master of what-is. Dasein having this manner of being is *in-sistent*, it sticks obstinately to what is directly presented to it by an entity, and actually resists any attempt to inquire into that which renders all disclosure possible. We tried earlier to grasp the openness of Dasein in terms of the notion of existing. Heidegger points out now that ex-sistent Dasein is at the same time in-sistent.

In-sisting, man is delivered up to error. "Man's drifting from the mystery to the practicable and from one practicability to the next, always missing the mystery, is *erring* [*das Irren*]" (p. 317). "Error is the essential counter-essence [*das wesentliche Gegenwesen*] of the original essence of truth" (p. 317). This original essence shows itself as untruth in the sense of hiddenness. It is because error stems from the essence of truth that man is able to advance from error to this essence. "Then the reason why the essence of truth is bound up with the truth of essence stands revealed" (p. 319). This takes place in the course of that thinking which reflects on Being itself. Heidegger calls it "philosophy" here. Later, he will expressly set philosophy off against thinking.

We may cite, in conclusion, Heidegger's comments summing up the course taken by the inquiry. "The present essay leads the question concerning the essence of truth beyond the confines of our accustomed ways of defining as we find them in the prevailing concept of essence and helps us to consider whether the question of the essence of truth is not at the same time necessarily the question of the truth of essence. In the concept of 'essence,' however, philosophy thinks of Being. By tracing the inner possibility of the correctness of a statement back to the ex-sistent freedom of letting-be as the very basis of that statement, and by suggesting that the essential origin of this basis is to be found in concealment and error, we may have indicated that the nature of truth is not just the empty 'generality' of some 'abstract' universality; it is something singular that lies concealed in the unique history of the disclosure of the 'meaning' of that which we call Being and which we have long been accustomed to think of only as what-is-in-totality" (p. 322).

The third step of this thinking, namely, the transformation in the sentence "The essence of truth is the truth of essence," is not taken here; this was to be done in a second lecture.

When we try to compare the above with *Being and Time*, we find that in *Being and Time* the traditional concept of truth is put into question, as is the traditional view that truth has its locus in judgment. In the context of the new concept of Dasein as being-in-the-world, truth is conceived as the truth of existence, that is, as resoluteness. In other words, resoluteness in the sense of un-closedness is the presupposition of man's relation to entities, in which relation entities become accessible, appear, show themselves as true. In the lecture on truth the situation is altered. To put it roughly, thinking does not, starting from Dasein, proceed in the direction of truth but, rather, Dasein and its relation to what-is are seen in a new light from the point of view of truth. The relation of man to beings is exhibited as overtness, or being-open-to, and overt-ness itself is thought of as freedom, that is, as the letting-be of entities in the sense of letting oneself into (*sich einlassen auf*, yielding or consenting to) what is. This refers to the unconcealed (*Unverborgene*), in which alone such a letting-into can take place. It is true that here Heidegger still speaks in terms of beings in their totality and, to that extent, is still reminiscent of the mode of interpreting in metaphysics, which seeks to think about what-is as a whole. However, this way of interpreting is at the same time put into question when Heidegger says in the last section, "as the quest for this truth, philosophy has in itself a twofold nature. Its meditations have the calm dignity of gentleness, which does not deny itself the concealedness of what-is-in-totality. At the same time they have the 'open resolve' of rigorousness which, while not shat-tering the concealment, forces its essence whole and intact into the openness of comprehension, and so into its own truth" (pp. 320–21). This means going beyond metaphysics, for the thinking of the concealedness in the essence of truth is something that has never been attempted by metaphysics.

We said at the outset that Heidegger's procedure is guided by a questioning that is in itself twofold: inquiry into Being and inquiry into truth. This duality emerges explicitly in the sentence, "the essence [Wesen, essence, nature] of truth is the truth of essence." This is not a playful inversion, nor is it an appropriation of the traditional essentialistic philosophy of the Platonic type, but is meant to indicate that we can think what truth is only when we try to think of Being itself. Truth of essence is truth of Being, as Heidegger says (in the part of the Note added later): "The subject of the sentence, if at all this unfortunate grammatical category must still be employed, is the truth of essence [Wesen, essencing, be-ing]" (Wegmarken, p. 96). Essence itself should be thought of in a verbal sense. "Truth means concealing-sheltering [Bergen] while bringing about a clearing [lichtend, making light] as the basic characteristic of Being" (Wegmarken, p. 96). Truth is comprehended in its inmost sense when we try to think of it as the clearing (Lichtung) which first lets everything that is make its appearance, emerge. It is this clearing that Heidegger will be reflecting upon in the coming years and decades. Let us now discuss the successive stations on this path.

Art and Aletheia ("The Origin of the Work of Art," 1935)

In order to discuss the problem of the essay "The Origin of the Work of Art"*[14] let us select a few key sentences from the text and try to elucidate them in a coherent way. This will show what significance *aletheia* has in Heidegger's interpretation of art. These are the sentences:

(1) In the work of art the truth of an entity has set itself to work (p. 36).
(2) The setting up of a world and the setting forth of earth are two essential features in the work-being of the work (p. 48).
(3) The nature of truth is, in itself, the primal conflict in which that open center is won within which what is, stands, and from which it sets itself back into itself (p. 55).
(4) This shining, joined in the work, is the beautiful. *Beauty is one way in which truth occurs as unconcealedness* (p. 56).
(5) Preserving the work, as knowing, is a sober standing-

* Unless otherwise mentioned, page references in this chapter are to *Poetry, Language, Thought*, translated by Albert Hofstadter (New York: Harper & Row, 1971).

within the extraordinary awesomeness of the truth that is happening in the work (pp. 67–68).

(6) *All art*, as the letting happen of the advent of the truth of what is, is, as such, *essentially poetry* (p. 72).

The text begins with the announcement of the central concern here, namely, discovering that origin, arising out of which a work of art becomes a work of art. "Origin here means that from and by which something is what it is and as it is" (p. 17). To think about what and how something is, is to think about its nature. What the inquiry seeks to find out is the origin of the work of art. Thus we are concerned not with an aesthetic discussion about the work of art, not with some reflections or inspired ideas about it, but with a strict question, a question which we usually avoid facing by remarking that, after all, this is something well known. For, works of art are there simply because artists have produced them. Consequently, the artist is in a way the origin. But on the other hand, is it not the case that an artist is an artist because he has produced these works? Does not his being an artist then depend on the works? "The artist is the origin of the work. The work is the origin of the artist" (p. 17). That is a strange reciprocal reference. Is not art the origin of both—the work and the artist? But what is art? We are unable to proceed further without drawing the nature of art into our questioning. And yet, in order to find out what art is we must hold on to works of art. Heidegger has thus, at the very outset, placed us within a circular inquiry and at that, too, not quietly but explicitly declaring it to be prerequisite to our procedure. We should not be afraid of this circularity. We must, on the contrary, expressly plant ourselves in it, endure and sustain it. Perhaps this circularity of procedure is involved in all hermeneutic problems. There is no question here of infringing on the well-known dictum requiring us to avoid circularity, as we know it from logic, because here nothing is sought to be proved or inferred. We are concerned with letting something be seen; here, the closer we are led up to the matter, the more we are able to glimpse. This is just what happens in the circular movement which we must perform: from the work to art, from art to the work.

When we try to grasp the work of art, we find that we can approach it by way of the fact that it is a thing. Heidegger analyzes the various familiar attempts at defining a thing: a thing as the bearer of properties; a thing as the unity of the manifold of sense-data; a thing as formed stuff. He distinguishes the following: the mere thing, that is, something which is naturally there; a thing meant for use (the utensil made by man); and the work (in the sense of a work of art). When we try to see what is essential in these distinctions, we find that the above-mentioned interpretations do not take us far. Even the form-content schema is of no help. Like the other explanations, it is "an encroachment upon the thing-being of the thing" (p. 30). This encroachment is not something willed by us; we find exhibited in it the history of metaphysics, with its attempts at thinking about beings.

We must try to discover another way. Heidegger is concerned not so much with showing us that these attempts do not take us far (although this also plays a part), as with drawing our attention to the fact that in all current definitions, like those of a thing, the history of metaphysics is already at work, without our taking this into account. We mean to approach the facts quite directly, without any bias, while taking over, nonetheless, metaphysical interpretations of what is. Heidegger is engaged in a standing debate with metaphysics. He is in no way concerned with resolving into a higher synthesis the solutions or interpretations given by metaphysics, but rather with finding a path which, at the same time, represents a turning away from metaphysics. What we witness here is the quest of a path.

In order to find out what a utensil is, Heidegger adopts a curiously roundabout way. He takes an artistic representation—van Gogh's picture of a peasant's shoes. From this picture we learn something of the world of the peasant—his work, his hardships, his worries and exertions. All of a sudden, we are given a new definition of the nature of a utensil: *reliability*. What does this mean? And how can we justify this definition? Let us begin by putting into relief that concept of a utensil which regards it exclusively in terms of its serviceability, as was done in fact in *Being and Time*, though the discussion there also went a little beyond this. The inquiry into the worldhood of the world proceeded by way of destination to what is most peculiar to the environing world.

The conception of a utensil solely in terms of serviceability grasps it merely from the point of view of its utility. That is quite a consistent and obvious way of understanding it. But it does not take us far. If we do not move beyond it, we get to know the utensil only in its "desolation," cut off from its ground, as pure instrument. But then, is the utensil not in fact a pure instrument? Is its function as a means not manifested when we regard it as such? Do we not overburden it by attributing more to it? What can be meant by "reliability"? Is it that through the utensil we are admitted into a world and that the utensil, at the same time, gives us access to the earth, which is part of a world (we might provisionally call it "Nature")? We do not intend to examine here whether this function is fulfilled by all utensils or whether there is some implement which may be called pre-eminent in this respect. In the example chosen by Heidegger, the shoes of a peasant, there is also present, along with the shoes, the realm of labor as the world of the peasant, and with it goes also that in which this world unfolds, the earth in the sense of *physis*.

The concept of earth emerges as something new in Heidegger's thinking about this time, presumably in the context of his exposition of the poetry of Hölderlin, especially from 1934–35 on. In this semester, Heidegger gave his first great lecture course on Hölderlin, with its exciting interpretation of the hymns "Germanien" and "Der Rhein," a lecture course which also dealt with the problem of the relationship between poetry and philosophy.

The quintessence of the excursus on utensils is that by way of a work of art (van Gogh's picture) we have learned what it is that makes a utensil what it is: reliability. The utensil-character has become manifest (not in the course of handling the implement, but through being represented in a work of art), exhibiting also what really matters in a work as such. The work makes manifest what a certain entity is. Making manifest is another expression for letting something make its appearance. In the work of art, something—in our case, a specified entity—makes its appearance: It shows itself in respect to what it is. With this stepping-into-appearance, however, we have the first allusion to the realm of *aletheia* as unhiddenness. So it is not surprising when Heidegger says, "if there occurs in the work a disclosure of a particular being, disclosing what and how it is, then there is here an occurrence, a happening of truth at work" (p. 36). "Disclosure of a particular being, disclosing what and how it is"—this means that an entity becomes accessible in its essential nature. In this case, it means that a thing becomes familiar in terms of its reliability, that this reliability is expressly experienced. When this occurs, it is nothing short of a happening of truth. "Truth" means here letting beings become accessible in their essence.

From the work we come to know what the thing really is as a utensil. At the same time, we come to know what the work is, namely, what happens in the work and through it: the becoming accessible of an entity with regard to what it is. Obviously, we can handle a utensil even before seeing it represented in a work of art, but it is the work of art that leads us to comprehend the utensil in its being a utensil, to see, thus, what it is that makes it into a utensil. This presupposes, of course, that we do not simply stare at the work of art and content ourselves with establishing similarities between what is represented in the work of art and what we have already seen before, but that we enter into what is going on here. That is just what is stated in the first key sentence chosen by us: "In the work of art the truth of an entity has set itself to work. 'To set' means here: to bring to a stand" (p. 36).

With this, we are at the center of Heidegger's exposition of art, although we have not yet expressly grasped the nature of this center as such. The course of the inquiry makes it clear that we cannot comprehend the work so long as we cling to the thingly substructure, so to speak. It is not through the substructure that the work becomes a work, but because something exhibits itself in it which was not seen before. It is this phenomenon of showing it-self that we must investigate if we wish to bring out the special feature of the work, as compared with the utensil and to the mere thing. In other words, if the work of art is a setting of truth to work, we must examine how truth is to be considered in its connection with the nature of the work.

For this purpose an analysis of a work is again carried out, that of a Greek temple. While it was possible in the previous example to understand art in terms of a depiction and to think that the work fulfills its function by representing something, we cannot do that in this case. A temple copies nothing, represents nothing. And yet, here too something goes on: "It is the temple-work that first fits together and at the same time gathers around itself the unity of those paths and relations in which birth and death, disaster and blessing, victory and disgrace, endurance and decline acquire the shape of destiny for human being" (p. 42). The relations men tioned here constitute what we call "world." It is within these relations that men live and hold themselves in this epoch. They determine both their approach to what is and their self-understanding. However, the temple does not bring to light merely the characteristic features of the world. It is erected at a favored site. By standing there, it pointedly brings the site itself to light, lets it shine forth. To put it more precisely, it is not the site as just another place but is that on which all locations are grounded, what the Greeks conceived as *physis*—in the language of Heidegger, the "earth." Since the peculiar character of a work of art consists in bringing world and earth to each other and to let them expressly emerge together, it is necessary to offer a more detailed account of these two.

"The world is not the mere collection of the countable or uncountable, familiar and unfamiliar things that are just there. But neither is it a merely imagined framework added by our representation to the sum of such given things. The *world worlds*, and is more fully in being than the tangible and perceptible realm in which we believe ourselves to be at home. World is never an object that stands before us and can be seen. World is the ever-nonobjective to which we are subject as long as the paths of birth and death, blessing and curse keep us transported into Being. Wherever those decisions of our history that relate to our very being are made, are taken up and abandoned by us, go unrecognized and are rediscovered by new inquiry, there the world worlds" (pp. 44–45).

Ordinarily, we seek to understand the world as the sum of

objects known to us or those we can possibly know. This is rejected here. We cannot grasp the peculiar feature of the world of
the Middle Ages by adducing the objects known in that period.
How then can we arrive at a comprehension of the world? When
we come to know the manner in which entities become accessible
to men in a particular epoch or, to put it differently, the kind of
openness in which men stand, so that entities may be encountered
in a corresponding fashion. The openness is not something tangible;
it cannot be objectified, for it is itself nothing objective.

We come closer to what Heidegger thinks here if we try to
think of the world as the specific mode of openness on which all
our relations to beings are based. The openness concerns not only
the nonhuman entities encountered by man but even his self-
understanding, his understanding of his fellow men and his understanding of the divine as well. Because world consists in the
happening of openness and because the work of art "sets up a
world" (p. 45), that is why Heidegger can say, "The work holds
open the Open of the world" (p. 45). In the work of art this
openness expressly shines forth.

Setting up (Aufstellen) a world is one principal feature of the
work; the other characteristic also concerns a setting or putting
(Stellen), namely, a setting-forth (Her-stellen, making, pro-ducing).
This suggests the practical idea of mechanical production. As a
matter of fact, a work does involve such activities as executing a
task, fashioning something, altering it and the like. But this is not
what Heidegger has in mind when he speaks of putting-forth. An
example may make this clear. In the usual sense of producing
(Herstellen) it is a question of working up some material for the
purpose of preparing some equipment or tool. Here the main thing
is to see that the stuff of which it is made does not make its appearance, does not obtrude, but is taken up entirely in the function
which it is meant to perform. The steel of the knife should appear
not as steel but as a cutting edge especially suited to the purpose of
cutting, so that we may devote ourselves entirely to this activity,
without having to attend to the material.

This disappearance (withdrawal) of the stuff in favor of its
utility, in the production of a utensil, is contrasted with the way in

which the "stuff" stands out in a work of art. This applies to sculpture as well as, in a different form, to painting and architecture. In the case of the temple, this concerns not only the marble of which it was built but, at the same time, letting the earth, the *physis*, stand out also. It is this letting-step-forth of the earth that is thought here in the notion of setting forth or making. This is not a making in which something very new, unusual or sensational is produced, but one which makes us free for that on which we ever stand, on which we always move, or, in a word, dwell. The earth makes its appearance because the work—the temple—sets itself back into it.

In a brief comment, Heidegger points out that, although the scientific-calculating mode of experience can objectify the earth and thus have it available for control, yet this way of dealing with it does not by any means make the earth comprehensible as the earth, that is, as our dwelling place. The very possibility that the scientific-technical mode of dealing with the earth might lead to devastating results in respect to dwelling makes us see this quite plainly. This is not surprising, because there is no such thing as the concept of "dwelling" or "sojourn" in the conceptual apparatus of natural science. In contrast with Nature as a source of energy for our exploitation, Heidegger sets the earth as that which cannot be opened up, as that which is the undisclosable, which is discerned and preserved as such in the work of art.

"To set forth the earth means to bring it into the Open as the self-secluding" (p. 47). Heidegger adds immediately, "This setting forth of the earth is achieved by the work as it sets itself back into the earth" (p. 47). We arrive, thus, at the second key sentence: "The setting up of a world and the setting forth of earth are two essential features in the work-being of the work" (p. 48).

It is by virtue of setting up a world and setting forth the earth that the work is a work. The resting-in-itself of a work, which distinguishes it from a mere thing and from a utensil, happens in both these modes of setting. But is rest something that can happen? Is that not a self-contradiction? "Only what is in motion can rest. The mode of rest varies with the kind of motion. In motion as the mere displacement of a body, rest is, to be sure, only the limiting case of motion. Where rest includes motion, there can exist a repose which is an inner concentration of motion, hence a highest state of agitation, assuming that the mode of motion requires such a rest" (p. 48).

In order to understand repose, we must bring to greater prominence the agitation with which we are here concerned. Heidegger accomplishes this by examining the tension between world and earth, by exposing this tension more distinctly. The tension here is to be understood in the sense of a strife, that is, a conflict which does not abolish the opponents or cancel their opposition by taking them up into a higher synthesis, as in the case of dialectical thought, for instance, but which lets it remain as a standing tension. In his own way, Heraclitus has already given expression to this idea.

The op-position of world and earth first exhibits itself as the opposition between what opens itself up and something that shuts itself in. In the world, we have the realm of openness, in which our decisions can unfold. Historical worlds are distinguished from one another according to the modes of openness characterizing them, as we saw earlier. This is not difficult to follow, but the thought of the earth is somewhat startling. "The earth is the spontaneous forthcoming of that which is continually self-secluding and to that extent sheltering and concealing" (p. 48). In this description, there is a ring of the Greek experience of *physis*. That which steps out of itself and shelters itself back into itself, unfolds itself and takes back into itself what is thus unfolded—such is earth as it is thought here.

In his interpretation of Hölderlin's poem "As on a holiday . . .," this is what Heidegger says about *physis*: "φύσις is the emerging and the coming forth, the opening up of itself, which while going forth into emergence, at the same time goes back and thus conceals itself in respect of that which gives to each present entity its coming-to-presence [*Anwesung*] . . . φύσις is the coming-forth returning-into-itself and is a name for the coming-to-presence of that which lingers in the coming forth occurring in this manner as the open" (*Erläuterungen zu Hölderlins Dichtung*, p. 55). Here, it is true, *physis* is thought in such a wide sense that it

becomes a name for Being, for that which, in the opposition of
world and earth, is held apart in tension in the essay on the work
of art.

There is no world without earth, no openness which cannot
so to speak install itself, settle down, on the earth. "The world
grounds itself on the earth" (p. 49). But the earth is at the same
time that which exhibits itself in the open and that which we
come to see as the place where world grounds itself, where it installs itself. This place should not be regarded as an empty space
but as the abode in which man settles down. Heidegger formulates
the mutual dependence of world and earth as follows: "The earth
cannot dispense with the Open of the world if it itself is to appear
as earth in the liberated surge of its self-seclusion. The world,
again, cannot soar out of the earth's sight [float away from the
earth] if, as the governing breadth and path of all essential destiny,
it is to ground itself on a resolute foundation" (p. 49).

In a work this strife is brought to a head, carried out to its
end. We cannot here go into the question of whether this element
of conflict, which could be brought into view in an exemplary manner in the case of a temple, is present in the same way in all the
arts.

The course of the reflection returns now to the assertion
quoted above that in art the truth of what is, is set into a work.
Heidegger has completed the circular movement of understanding.
We see, of course, that we are not dealing with a mere circling
in the sense of coming back to the same point again and again. As
a result of what has been stated up till now about the work of
art, we are in a position to approach the discussion of the nature
of truth with a new insight. In addition, ideas from the lecture on
truth are again taken up in a succinct way. *Aletheia* itself now becomes the principal theme. "Unconcealedness is, for thought, the
most concealed thing" (p. 51), or as we have it in the essay
"Hegel and the Greeks," "'Ἀλήθεια is the enigma itself—the matter
of thinking" (*Wegmarken*, p. 268).

Heidegger goes on to show at this point how thinking about
unconcealedness is by no means a misguided or even odd enterprise;
how, on the contrary, it is only when it is already presupposed that

the matter shows itself (compare Chapter 5), that the condition which has been laid down as the criterion of truth, the correspondence of knowledge with the matter—which is then expressed in a sentence—is itself possible. Truth as correctness or rightness presupposes that entities stand in the open, that between thing and man something in the nature of an openness reigns, that man is open for the thing and that openness reigns between man and man. Heidegger has set this forth in the lecture course of 1937–38 entitled "Logik."

The inquiry into unhiddenness leads to a questioning back into what has remained unthought in the traditional conception of truth, and is always presupposed in it. This has been specially discussed by Heidegger in the lectures just mentioned, where he has also shown that the Greeks experienced unconcealedness as the ground of truth, but without putting it expressly into question. This also made it possible later for this ground not to be kept in mind, to be indeed buried and covered over so thoroughly that no need was felt any longer to lay it open again. To awaken this need, to make us discern the necessity of such need—this is what is at stake for Heidegger. In the present text Heidegger says, ". . . it is not we who presuppose the unconcealedness of beings; rather, the unconcealedness of beings (Being) puts us into such a condition of being that in our representation we always remain installed within and in attendance upon unconcealedness. Not only must that in *conformity* with which a cognition orders itself be already in some way unconcealed. The entire *realm* in which this 'conforming to something' goes on must already occur as a whole in the unconcealed; and this holds equally of that *for* which the conformity of a proposition to fact becomes manifest" (p. 52).

Unhiddenness as clearing is the presupposition (that which has been posited already), which is not a supposition expressly made by us, but one in which we are rather transposed, though without actually noticing it because we always cling to entities which are manifest to us.

Since it offers an open space, "This open center is therefore not surrounded by what is; rather, the lighting center itself encircles all that is, like the Nothing which we scarcely know. That which is can only be, as a being, if it stands within and stands out within what is lighted in this clearing. Only this clearing grants and guarantees to us humans a passage to those beings that we ourselves are not, and access to the being that we ourselves are. Thanks to this clearing, beings are unconcealed in certain changing degrees" (p. 53).

Because this clearing is not thought of, that is, not noticed, as a clearing—it is apparently enough that we grasp that which appears in it—therefore, Heidegger can say that it withdraws itself, that it is a concealment, the concealment of itself. This character exhibits itself in two ways, which Heidegger conceives as refusal and dissembling.

What is "refusal" meant to convey? When we say of an entity only that it is, we seem to dispense with everything else—what is present (the present entity) seems actually to resist further determination. This is what "refusal" means here. But in this refusal itself we have the incipience of the reversal which leads us to disengage ourselves from entities and to look at the clearing itself. A contrariety is inherent within refusal: denial and promise, which should not, however, be thought of in terms of human activity.

What is the meaning of "dissembling"? That an entity thrusts itself before another, that we take the one for the other, which means that here we have an indication of the possibility of error, deception, oversight.

Refusal has no doubt a certain priority, whereas dissembling is a secondary mode of concealing. The important point is that concealment is not something that is simply to be abolished and overcome, as though we might draw a concealed object from its hiding place and then have it at our disposal. We do not have concealment in our control but are, on the contrary, always exposed to it. Being exposed to concealment is described by Heidegger as the denial-permeated, denial-dominated nature of truth which he formulates as follows: "Truth, in its nature, is un-truth" (p. 54; compare p. 88 above). Unconcealedness as clearing involves denial in the mode of concealing. This points to the fact that in truth itself, as thus conceived, a strife prevails. The clearing is what is contended for, striven for, in this strife. Truth is itself a happening, namely, the

happening of the conflict between unconcealedness and concealment. The third key sentence, we may recall, is: "The nature of
truth is, in itself, the primal conflict in which that open center is
won within which what is, stands, and from which it sets itself
back into itself" (p. 55).

Here we come upon the connection between truth and Being,
without being yet in a position, however, to develop it expressly.
These remarks are meant to bring out Heidegger's efforts to gain
insight into *aletheia*. Although it renders possible all access to what
is as well as the fact that entities show themselves, *aletheia* itself
nonetheless remains enigmatic. As Heidegger explains in the lecture
course on logic, unconcealedness is to be thought of as the range of
vision or horizon within which the inquiry into what is becomes
possible. This horizon must first flash up in order that what stands
in it may become expressly visible, but at the same time it must
itself be in a way disregarded. Heidegger's thought circles round
this enigmatic state of affairs. He does not provide any final solution but, instead, constantly tries out new approaches. All talk about
aletheia thus remains provisional. This is something we must not
forget, otherwise we shall turn this thinking, which regards itself
primarily as inquiry, as the paving of a path, into some kind of
dogmatics. Doing so means to put an end to the passion of thinking
or at least to render it quiescent and innocuous, which is even worse
than crass incomprehension. "Provisional" (from the Latin *provisio*,
foresight) does not at all mean temporary or even indifferent. It
contains rather the idea of anticipating, in the sense of searching, of
looking out, for something. We can come closer to that which keeps
Heidegger's thinking on the move only when we understand Heidegger's circling round *aletheia* as an ever-renewed search for fresh
starts, prompting us to a quest of our own, and only when in these
approaches we become directly aware of the conflict between clearing and concealment, and thus do not cling to the definitions but
notice how they have been arrived at and how far they take us and
what they perhaps fail to grasp.

Prior to the fundamental discussion of the problem of truth,
we mentioned the strife between world and earth, and just now we
encountered the strife within truth itself. How are the two to be
brought together?

We tend to equate the world with the clearing and the earth with concealment. In the course of the discussion it becomes apparent that the characteristic feature of the world is openness, that a change of our world is equivalent to a change in this manifestness. Heidegger, however, sees the character of conflict within world and earth themselves. In the world, the opponency exhibits itself in this that, through the clearing that rules in it, the world provides the possibility of decisions. "Every decision, however, bases itself on something not mastered, something concealed, confusing; else it would never be a decision" (p. 55).

We can perhaps paraphrase this so: By thinking of world as a specific openness, the opposition between openness and concealment is not abolished. The openness, in which decisions are made, does not in any way relieve these decisions of their gravity. Furthermore, this openness is not some kind of controlling power, needing only an executive vehicle in order to prevail. Such a language of power is not compatible with the phenomena. The openness of the world generates a certain relationality with entities; what occurs in it is altogether undetermined. In this indeterminateness lies also that which remains unmastered in the sense of the concealed.

In the case of the earth, we mentioned at the very beginning its inherent contrariety: rising, coming forth and returning into itself. Clearing and concealment—the primal strife of truth—dominates throughout world as well as earth. This primal conflict is a happening. Where is it to be found? Heidegger says here only that one way in which truth happens has its seat in the work of art. Other ways are mentioned later.

The two moments of work-being, setting up a world and setting forth of earth, constitute, at the same time, "the fighting of the battle in which the unconcealedness of beings as a whole, or truth, is won" (p. 55).

We must get rid of one misconception straightway, that by representing something the work gives expression to what is true, a misunderstanding of *mimesis* which has long dominated the theory of art. What is meant here is not what appears so obvious to us, that in a picture and through it the matter itself becomes evident. This may be quite true at a certain level and it may even be a legitimate requirement, but here what is attempted is to lay bare a more fundamental level. "Thus in the work it is truth, not only something true that is at work" (p. 56). This means that it is unconcealedness as such that occurs, not merely the disclosure of certain entities.

Is this the case with all works of art or only with exceptional ones? A work represents in the proper sense only that which is, for the common understanding, something uncommon. In a work of this kind it is the unconcealedness of what is in its totality that shines forth. That is what makes such works epoch-making. We now come upon the fourth key sentence: "This shining, joined in the work, is the beautiful. *Beauty is one way in which truth occurs as unconcealedness*" (p. 56).

The beautiful is thus not explained in terms of subjective experience, of how the work affects a subject, but in terms of the openness that becomes manifest in a work of art, of the basic phenomenon of unconcealedness. It is true that unconcealedness cannot be grasped objectively, for it is nothing objective in character but makes the appearing of all that appears in the first place possible. Nevertheless, how an entity makes its appearance within this unconcealedness can certainly be pictured and grasped, and it is by way of this stepping-into-appearance that we gain an indication of the sway of unconcealedness itself, that is to say, of Being. This happens, according to Heidegger, in the work; the sway of unconcealedness gives to the work its beauty, that is, its character of shining forth. In it, this shining itself makes its appearance, though in such a peculiar way that ordinarily we do not notice it at all, with our eyes always set upon just that which appears, that is, the particular entity and what comes to pass with it. When Heidegger speaks of "the way in which truth occurs [*west*]," this means how truth *is* as truth, how unconcealment *is* as unconcealment. Why then does he not say "is" instead of "occurs"? Because, ordinarily, we use "is" for the being of things—the table is big, the mountain is precipitous—and for ways of behaving—deception is common, loyalty is touching. Here, however, we are not concerned with such things or phenomena but with a nonobjective presencing (*An-Wesenheit*), an unobjective happening.

This key sentence terminates an old controversy running

through history, namely, the question of whether beauty has anything to do with truth or whether the beautiful must be excluded
from the realm of the true. This does not in any way mean that
beauty is the only possible mode of experiencing truth, only that it
is *one* possible way.

The investigation which was to be devoted to the work of art
appears to have shifted from the work as such to a consideration of
truth. It is time that we go into the peculiar character of a work
as something made or created, so that its difference from the merely
produced character of a handicraft may become visible. This consideration does not by any means lead us away from the problem of
truth but, on the contrary, demands a reserved putting-into-question
of truth.

"Of what nature is truth, that it can be set into work, or even
under certain conditions must be set into work, in order to be *as*
truth?" (p. 57). In the traditional approach to the problem, the
question of the connection between beauty and truth is raised at
the end. With Heidegger, on the contrary, the starting point for
the determination of the work of art is the happening of truth, and
the work of art is itself placed in the service of this happening,
indeed, becomes itself accessible because of this happening.
The discussion of this problem moves into fundamentals in the
third part of the essay, entitled "Truth and Art."

"In unconcealedness, as truth, there occurs also the other 'un-'
of a double restraint or refusal. Truth occurs as such in the opposition of clearing and double concealing" (p. 60), namely, of refusal
and dissembling. A-*letheia* shelters *Lethe* within itself. The strife
going on within truth itself leads to the contest for such a thing as
openness, in which what is manifest makes its appearance. As Heidegger formulates it, openness must establish (*einrichten*) itself in
its open. "Hence there must always be some being in this Open,
something that is, in which the openness takes its stand and attains
its constancy" (p. 61). The work is an entity of this kind. Other
ways in which truth establishes itself are: the deed that founds a
political state, by which life in community is given a foundation;
the essential sacrifice, in the sense of standing up for one's fellow
men; and quite a different one, lastly, thinking itself, for which

truth is what is most questionable. In contrast, science is understood as moving into a realm already opened up. If a scientist himself achieves such an opening up, then he is also a philosopher.

A change has taken place here in the approach to the problem and to the way of posing it, in which the inquiry does not proceed from art to truth but in which we seek to gain insight into art from the point of view of truth—the decisive contribution of Heidegger to the entire thematics of art which, to be sure, was so far hardly understood. This altered approach shows the work as being demanded by truth itself, in the sense of the installation of truth, its taking a concrete form.[15]

"Because it is in the nature of truth to establish itself within that which is, in order thus first to become truth, therefore the impulse toward the work lies in the nature of truth as one of truth's distinctive possibilities by which it can itself occur as being in the midst of beings" (p. 62).

This state of affairs might be understood in the sense that a certain relationality to what-is was already there and only needed the work in order to become visible. This is not the sense in which it is thought of here. What is really brought forth in the work is not this particular form for which the material is provided. It is rather the peculiar character of relationality, of having reference to entities (openness), that expressly takes place in the work. "Where this bringing forth expressly brings the openness of beings, or truth, that which is brought forth is a work" (p. 62). What shines out in the work of Rembrandt or in that of Cézanne or Kafka are such possibilities of openness, through which what is in its entirety becomes familiar to us in a different way, because an entity can be encountered by us as something that is only in so far as it stands in the open. This is one of Heidegger's basic insights.

There is no doubt that this interpretation of the work of art has opened a new path in the discussion about art, though how far it can be made to yield results depends on us. It may be good that we do not, to begin with, take this path, for doing so presupposes the effort of thinking. On the other hand, it is also possible that we might appropriate the basic idea of truth being set into the work without seeing, at the same time, the specific tension between world and earth, suggested to Heidegger by his starting out from the Greeks and from Hölderlin.[16]

In the "earth," a word which is hard to think of appropriately, there is gathered together for Heidegger what we so inadequately seek to conceive of as material and what is necessarily part of the work of art, though in a different way, of course, in the plastic and graphic arts than in poetry and music. The place of the concept of form is taken by figure or shape (Gestalt), which at first seems to be similar to it. But figure is not the look, which we happen to have discovered, of what is pictured in the work; it is rather the way in which truth is fitted or joined together in its appearing, which Heidegger calls the "rift" (Riss), the coming into view of the strife of world and earth.

The created character of the work is the "conflict's being fixed in place in the figure by means of the rift" (p. 66). The next statement, "Createdness here is itself expressly created into the work," should not be understood as a question of the personality of the artist and of his originality. Being created should rather be understood as the openness which has been set into the work; how man, in the midst of entities, relates himself to them and how he understands even himself, all this is based on that specific openness.

The course of thought does not terminate with this discussion of what it is to be a work. A new line of questioning is started and it is governed by the idea of preserving. Through the work our ties and relations to the world and to the earth are changed. What is habitual undergoes a dislocation; in the work itself there is generated a shock so that the familiar ceases to be so; we are torn out of the accustomed. Not avoiding this change, not rendering it innocuous, to say nothing of hushing it up, but expressly experiencing it, this is for Heidegger preserving (Bewahren) the work. But this is not just a conserving and keeping in safe custody, protecting and taking care of it but, as the fifth key sentence declares: "Preserving the work, as knowing, is a sober standing-within [Inständigkeit, instancy] the extraordinary awesomeness of the truth that is happening in the work" (pp. 67–68).

In another formulation this is called "standing within the openness of beings that happens in the work" (p. 67). This standing-within is by no means a mere reception of something offered to us. It requires a special attitude in one who experiences it. This emerges clearly in what Heidegger says about instancy. Standing-within means closeness or nearness in the sense of familiarity, of being intimate, which is achieved only at the end of a process of development, so that our entire behavior is then sustained by this sense of intimacy. This is elucidated in the text in connection with knowing and willing. Experiencing the openness is a knowing, but not in the sense of merely getting to know something and representing it. It is rather a knowing that opens up to us, makes known to us, what we have to do, what we want. This intertwining of knowing and willing is the distinctive feature of Dasein. It is here that we have the occurrence of what is specific to existing, being admitted into unconcealment, into *aletheia*.

We have arrived at the point where Heidegger places us in the passage from the truth of beings to the truth of Being. We may also describe this as the transition from the experience of what is in its characteristic quality (exemplified in the analysis of the thing) to the experience of that which does not become thematic in metaphysics, namely, the clearing as such. That is *aletheia* as un-hiddenness, which itself remains hidden. Truth in the sense of *aletheia*, which first of all opens up in every case our being-familiar-with, which sustains and informs all our relationships, is from now on no longer thought of as truth of beings but as truth of Being. *Aletheia* and truth of Being are the same. Thrusting forward into this realm is, and remains always, something uncanny and awesome, for ordinarily we are wont to stick to what at the moment shows itself (an entity), or at most to this showing-itself (the mode in which entities appear), and thus lose all footing here, in this realm. We seem to be obliged to abandon all sense of familiarity; that is the change of the canny into the uncanny. This change is something we must endure, ride out, in preserving the work; that is the instancy required. It calls for a sober attitude, which means not letting oneself become confused and wavering by what is unwonted —also, not to hedge and to look for subterfuges in order to escape the uncanny, for that is what we habitually do.

To see what has come to pass in the work, to let oneself be

claimed by it, to be transformed by it and in this manner to endure and sustain it, that is what Heidegger means by preserving. So crucially important is this notion that we balk at it so long as we do not have a clear idea of what preserving means and how far removed it is from a reduction of the work to a merely subjective experience (compare p. 63 above).

The course of the discussion so far—from thing via the work to the interplay of world and earth, truth as the primal conflict, preserving as the experience of *aletheia*—makes it possible now to grasp the coherence of the intertwined phenomena and thus to come back to art, the initial subject of this inquiry. But this return at the same time paves the way for a new questioning.

"If art is the origin of work, this means that art lets those who naturally belong together in the work, the creator and the preserver, originate, each in his own nature" (p. 71). But art itself "was defined to begin with as the setting-into-work of truth" (p. 71). Setting-into-work is thought of in a twofold sense: as the establishing of truth itself in the figure, in the sense of the bringing forth of unconcealedness; and as the preserving of the truth that happens in the work. Thus Heidegger arrives at the definition of art: "the creative preserving of truth in the work" (p. 71). Letting truth in the sense of openness happen is called by Heidegger "poetry" (*Dichtung*). The sixth key sentence states: "*All art, as the letting happen of the advent of the truth of what is, is, as such, essentially poetry*" (p. 72). It is not an accident that this formulation rings simultaneously active and passive. Art does not arbitrarily create unconcealedness but becomes the place where truth may come to pass. Here perhaps there is a resonance of the thought which Heidegger has explained in his interpretation of Hölderlin: the idea of the poet as the mediator between gods and men.

The definition of art in terms of poetry offered by Heidegger does not at all mean reducing all the arts to poesy, but rather that, in all art, what is projected or composed (*gedichtet*) is truth in the sense of unconcealedness. Language itself (compare Chapter 9) is that through which entities are brought into the open. "Language itself is poetry in the essential sense. But since language is the happening in which for man beings first disclose themselves to him each time as beings, poesy—or poetry in the narrower sense—is the most original form of poetry in the essential sense" (p. 74).

The disclosure of entities that occurs in language is presupposed in all possible dealings we have with entities or, as we have it in the text, the other varieties of art "are an ever special poetizing within the clearing of what is, which has already happened unnoticed in language" (p. 74).

In a final step, what has been said so far is gathered up again and the determination of poetry as the founding of truth is elucidated. This founding is understood in a threefold sense: as *bestowing*, as *grounding* and as *beginning*. These three attributes may be briefly explained as follows. Through the transformation that occurs within the work of art, something novel is revealed, something that cannot be derived from what is already known. This novel something is an excess, a surplus—the granting of this surplus is bestowing.

In the bestowing of art there occurs a projecting, not in the sense of something arbitrarily concocted but so that the projecting makes possible for man precisely that within which he stands, his abode—that is, the grounding that occurs in art. The ground is hauled out, as it were. This is an ever-recurring idea in Heidegger which we have treated already in connection with the return to the beginnings. Thus, the first Greek thinkers laid the ground on which we stand, without being explicitly aware of it. This is further clarified by this definition of a beginning: "A genuine beginning, as a leap, is always a head start, in which everything to come is already leaped over, even if as something disguised" (p. 76).

The early thinking of the Greeks, which precedes metaphysical thinking, is for Heidegger, as we know, also the thinking that inaugurates the future, provided that we do not overleap it, pass it over or, in other words, forget our history.

"Always when that which is as a whole demands, as what is, itself, a grounding in openness, art attains to its historical nature as foundation. This foundation happened in the West for the first time in Greece. What was in the future to be called Being was set into work, setting the standard. The realm of beings thus opened up was then transformed into a being in the sense of God's creation.

This happened in the Middle Ages. This kind of being was again transformed at the beginning and in the course of the modern age. Beings became objects that could be controlled and seen through by calculation. At each time a new and essential world arose. At each time the openness of what is had to be established in beings themselves, by the fixing in place of truth in figure. At each time there happened unconcealedness of what is. Unconcealedness sets itself into work, a setting which is accomplished by art" (pp. 76–77).

We find sketched here the three decisive epochs which have been laid bare through the thinking of Heidegger and at the same time seen in their interrelatedness. The original nature of art is thought of by Heidegger in terms of the nature of truth. There happens in this labor of thought, as we tried to explain, a change in the thinking of truth itself, in the sense of revealing the enigmatic realm of *aletheia*. This seems to become evident in the very manner of speaking about truth. Ordinarily, Heidegger speaks of the truth of what is (beings) or of the truth of what is as such. But in the crucial passage the change "of the unconcealedness of what is" is thought as the unconcealedness "of Being" (p. 72). In this essay there occurs a transition from the truth of beings to the truth of Being or, in other words, from the truth of beings as such to that of unconcealedness, which necessarily precedes every manifestation of entities and which itself, on the other hand, needs entities to be able to appear as unconcealedness.

This essay is transitional also in respect to the attempt to think of world and earth in their interrelatedness, leading up subsequently to the idea of the fourfold (*Geviert*) (compare the lecture "The Thing"). It is also the essay in which *aletheia* itself—which was, for Heidegger, the objective of the quest of thought from the very beginning—is inquired after, which means thought about, more radically. We are in the period preparatory to the turn (*Kehre*), the change in thinking which understands Dasein in terms of Being and no longer, as in *Being and Time*, starts with Dasein in order to arrive at Being. Our aim here was to show that to inquire into art (as the origin of the work) is at the same time to inquire into Being (world and earth), as well as into *aletheia*—and that, too, in its transitional character.

30. Heidegger with Georges Braque, Varengeville, 1955

31. Jean-Paul Sartre

32. René Char

33. Heidegger with Jean Beaufret at the cottage

34. Heidegger with Walter Biemel

35. Heidegger at Todtnauberg

37. Heidegger with his brother Fritz

. On the evening before Heidegger's seventieth birthday, 1959.
From right to left: Medard Boss, Heidegger, Mrs. Bröcker, Jean Beaufret,
Walter Biemel, Mrs. Boss, Heinrich Petzet, Walter Bröcker

38. Heidegger with his wife and sons, 1953

39. Heidegger writing "Art and Space," St. Gallen, 1968

40. Heidegger walking in his garden

The Humanity of Man ("Letter on 'Humanism,'" 1946)

The "Letter on 'Humanism'" was written in reply to questions raised by the French philosopher Jean Beaufret,* whom Heidegger went to see on his own initiative after the war. This was the beginning of a friendship which was to last for decades.

The topic which we place at the center of our account is how the humanity, the humanness, of man is to be considered.

We are accustomed to describing the inquiry into man, the concern about man, as humanism. In Paris there had appeared Sartre's short work "L'Existentialisme est un humanisme," in which Sartre, arguing against the Marxists' claim to represent humanism, aimed at setting forth existentialism as the true humanism. The question Beaufret put to Heidegger is: How can a new meaning be given to the word "humanism"? Heidegger poses the counterquestion: Is that necessary? With this, we are placed directly within the discussion as to the manner in which the nature of man is to be conceived.

---

* Written in 1946, this text was published in an enlarged version, with an interpretation of Plato's allegory of the cave, in 1947. At the suggestion of Beaufret, Heidegger was invited to colloquia at Cérisy in 1955 and at Thor, in Provence, where the poet René Char has his countryseat. Summaries of the meetings were published in 1968 and 1969 for the participants. Quotations in this chapter are from the English translation of this essay by Edgar Lohner, in *Philosophy in the Twentieth Century*, vol. 3, edited by William Barrett and H. D. Aiken (New York: Random House, 1962). This translation has in some cases been modified.

Heidegger's counterquestion can easily be misunderstood as suggesting that the inquiry into the nature of man is of no consequence to him. This is by no means the case. What, however, is fundamentally questionable for Heidegger is the attempt to define the nature of man from the point of view of humanism. Is not this attempt the most obvious one to make? It is indeed so, though it does not follow that it is also the most appropriate. This is the attempt which was carried out on the basis of metaphysics. In it the Roman starting point continues to provide the lead.

"In Rome we encounter the first humanism. It, thus, remains in its essence a specifically Roman phenomenon, born of the encounter between the Roman and Hellenistic cultures. The so-called Renaissance of the fourteenth and fifteenth centuries in Italy is a *renascentia romanitatis*. Since the *romanitas* is what matters, all we are concerned with is *humanitas* and for that reason, the Greek παιδεία. The Greek world, however, is always seen in its late form and this, in turn, is seen as Roman. Even the *homo romanus* of the Renaissance is seen in opposition to the *homo barbarus*. But the inhuman is now the alleged barbarism of the Gothic scholasticism of the Middle Ages. To humanism, historically understood, therefore, always belongs a *studium humanitatis*, which reaches back to antiquity and so always becomes a revival of the Greek world. This is shown in our humanism of the eighteenth century, which is sustained by Winckelmann, Goethe, and Schiller" (p. 275).

With this historical form of humanism, Heidegger contrasts that form of it which lies in interesting ourselves on behalf of man, but without being anchored in classical antiquity, as for example, Marxist humanism or Sartrian humanism. If what matters is "that man may become free for his humanity and find therein his dignity, then, depending on the particular concept of 'freedom' and the 'nature' of man, there are different kinds of humanism" (p. 275).

What constitutes a critique of the metaphysical basis of humanism? What, according to this form of humanism, is the distinctive feature of man? *Ratio*, which makes it possible for him to know and to act. He can set up goals for himself and can realize them by providing himself with the necessary means and by appropriate action. Why is this answer insufficient? Because, already underlying it there is a particular metaphysical interpretation of man, which is not at all seen by it as such. The question now is not whether Heidegger comes up with another assumption in opposition to the metaphysical assumption, for, in that case, it might be said, with Hegel, that one assumption is as legitimate as another, or as little. We have, rather, to search for that which is always implied and already presupposed in these assumptions, without being expressly considered. To be able to proceed further, it is necessary to have a clear understanding of the difficulty of philosophical discourse.

Plato's language—indeed, his thinking—is faced with the following difficulty: to make available to us by means of concrete examples that which cannot itself be concretely grasped but can only be thought. Plato's efforts are directed, after all, to bringing about a reversal from the visible to the invisible, in such fashion that the thinkable is seen to be the realm of what truly is and everything visible as being tainted with unreality, that is, with transitoriness. For example, Plato seeks to convey the Idea of the Good, the idea which has being-an-idea as its content, by means of the image of the sun—the sun whose light makes seeing possible and whose warmth promotes growth and blossoming in the realm of *physis*. Nevertheless, in order to understand what has been thought here, it is necessary to go beyond, transcend, the visible.

We find an analogous difficulty in Heidegger, which certainly does not mean that his thought is to be understood as Platonism, not even as reversed Platonism, as we have it in Nietzsche. In what does the difficulty lie? We habitually regard as real that which is, and as not real everything that is not and cannot be identified as a being. But then, what Heidegger thinks of as Being is by no means an entity, something that is. That is why, in his inaugural lecture, he could speak intentionally of Nothing, without thereby advocating nihilism. By "Nothing" he meant, on the contrary, that which, regarded from the point of view of beings, has apparently no being, but which is in reality intended to lead us to what is other than an entity—Being itself. How this is to be thought is a difficulty not finally resolved, but that it is at all something to be thought, that is what matters to Heidegger from the very beginning of his quest.

Now, in metaphysics such an attempt has apparently been

made. This is just what metaphysics means, the movement of thought beyond entities, reaching up to that which makes a being a being, something that is. In Aristotle's philosophical thought, this kind of thinking was realized for the first time in a manner which was nothing less than exemplary for posterity. The inquiry into beings *as* beings is the leading motif of metaphysics. In this inquiry we also find put forward, as a possible answer, the concept of a highest being, that is, of God. Heidegger has very clearly brought out the onto-theological character of the Aristotelian in-quiry. It is characteristic of the metaphysical procedure.

Heidegger is engaged in a continuous argument with meta-physics, which implies also that he is not satisfied with the pro-cedure of metaphysics, that he cannot find reassurance in it. Does it mean that he seeks to surmount metaphysics, somewhat as Fichte wanted to go beyond Kant's questioning by his rejection of the unknowability of the thing in itself? Not in the least. It is not a question of surpassing the highest being by setting up a yet higher entity, to explain the last principle by a finally ultimate ground. Rather, the main point is to attempt a turn, which is hard to carry out because it cannot be expressed in the language of meta-physics. For that very reason, when it is nevertheless accomplished, it is apt to be misunderstood. We might speak of this as a new project of interpreting that which is, but it must then be pointed out that this project is not an arbitrary assumption, not the play-ful excogitation of a new possibility. This is a project that has al-ready happened at the very beginning of philosophical thinking; Heidegger came across this project while seeking to comprehend this beginning, which came about prior to the rise of metaphysics, prior thus to Plato and Aristotle. Perhaps every genuine project is simul-taneously projecting and receiving. Only because Heidegger has carried out his project, a light dawned upon him in regard to the first thinkers and they acquired for him a prominent status. On the other hand, he was presumably enabled to carry out his project in the course of his struggle to gain insight into these thinkers, having been addressed by them and hearing their call. The unison with Heraclitus that we find in Heidegger is both a receiving and a be-stowal.

This can, of course, lead to the misconception that Heidegger is concerned only with transporting us back into the archaic, abandoning the "progress" of philosophical thought. This is a reproach that crops up repeatedly. The return to the early thinkers is a return to those questions in which that which is questionworthy flashes up for the first time. Here, according to Heidegger, something happens that is so stupendous that we can hardly stop wondering at it. That, as a matter of fact, this amazement has died down and that this stupendous event has been buried and repressed is one of those occurrences to which we must never resign ourselves, which we must, rather, combat ever anew.

What is the point of Heidegger's "pro-ject"? It is to make accessible the dimension which first of all enables a comprehension of what is, which, indeed, constitutes its basis. But it is not an inquiring back into the conditions of the possibility of knowledge in a subject in the sense of transcendental philosophy. In the latter, the subject stands at the center and everything that is not subject-like is conceived as object for a subject. This interpretation has led to a shift in emphasis which is decisive for modern metaphysics. Heidegger inquires into the problem of how entities can appear. Even this can be misunderstood as a question of appearing for a subject. Can there be an appearing unless we start out from a subject, hence without a being for whom something appears? Now, of course, even Plato talked about appearing. Conceiving an entity through the ἰδέα is a grasping of the appearance, the look, and in Plato, no subject-concept is involved. Heidegger's "pro-ject" should not, however, be understood as Platonic. What then is the point of an inquiry into appearing? We have already come across this in the lecture on truth where the ideas of being open and of openness are mentioned.

How does openness come about? When we formulate it in this way, we run the risk of seeking, in the manner of metaphysics, the causes and grounds of openness. Is it at all possible to inquire and seek in some other manner, without lapsing into mythological or metaphorical language? That, as a matter of fact, is what Heidegger attempts. That overtness is presupposed in speaking and making a judgment about entities has already been discussed. But what else is required so that there may be such overtness? In the lecture on truth a preliminary answer to this is attempted and stated in outline. In the essay on the work of art the thinking also revolved round truth, though in the sense of the primordial strife, of which the outcome is the "lighting center." Here, in the "Letter on 'Humanism,' " we have the same question, this time in connection with the determination of the nature of man. We must therefore examine how man is conceived in his relation to openness.

Let us begin with the concept of the *clearing*. The clearing is conceived as the place in which there happens a releasing, a setting-free, of entities, so that they may come to light. In the free space of the clearing, an entity comes to a stand, puts in its appearance. We easily tend to look upon the clearing as a kind of stage on which entities are presented to us. That is not how it is meant. For a release to be possible for entities, it is also necessary for man to open himself to entities, to ex-sist in the sense of standing out in the clearing. We mentioned the difficulty of the Platonic way of speaking, in which images taken from the sphere of the sensible are offered so that we can surmount the sensible. In Heidegger's case, where does the difficulty lie? It lies in this, that the aim is to lead us out of the objective manner of representing things, yet in doing so words are employed which can be understood in a merely objective sense and which are familiar to us from the objective sphere. For Heidegger, Being itself is never graspable objectively, because it is nothing objective. It is itself not an entity, but is that which may make comprehensible to us how we have access to entities at all. The answer to this "how" is: It is possible only because man, as *Da-sein* (being-there), stands in the open and endures the clearing that has come to pass. Standing in the open, entities, too, exhibit themselves as manifest. Still, how are we to consider, in connection with this, the moment of historicity which Heidegger has in view from the very beginning?

The clearing is not a neutral place where occurrences of all sorts may come to be represented, but is conceived, rather, as itself changing. What is the evidence for asserting this? It consists of the fact that in classical antiquity, in the Middle Ages, in the modern period, beings have been conceived in different ways, which means they have made their appearance in these different ways. We have no control over this change and cannot bring it about at will, according to Heidegger, but we can very well try to think about it, comprehend it in thought. Such an attempt is Heidegger's interpretation of the history of metaphysics as our history. A central point in this interpretation may be briefly touched upon. Metaphysics has not called into question its changing interpretations but has taken, from time to time, a particular position as the true one—for example, the interpretation of beings as ἰδέα, as ἐνέργεια, as *ens creatum*, as subject, as monad, as spirit, as will to power. In contrast, Heidegger attempts to question what goes on in these interpretations. He does so by asking: What is the nature of the particular clearing that has occurred at any given time, in which clearing do the philosophers stand, without expressly thinking of it *as* a clearing? Their thinking is directed toward entities. To think expressly about the change in the clearing as such, that is nonmetaphysical thinking according to Heidegger. To inquire into the Being that itself emerges in this change, without being expressly noticed (which, thus, in the very process of appearing also withdraws), is now the task of thinking (compare Chapter 10).

What have the above remarks to do with the humanness of man? To all appearances, they lead us away from this topic. The human character of human beings seems to be actually denied or at least forgotten. This impression is quite natural, for the human character of man is something that we are in the habit of seeing, and judging, in terms of his way of behaving and his doings, in his works and achievements, in his social behavior and his political actions. But it is not a question of any of this. And humanism, the concept by means of which we are used to understanding the nature of man, was expressly called into question, seen through and abandoned as a metaphysical manner of understanding man. As a matter of fact, however, the preceding account has prepared the ground on which, according to Heidegger, it now becomes possible to think about the nature of man. For, the nature of man can be defined only in terms of man's relationship to the clearing. As *Da-sein*, man is the being to whom it is given to stand in the clearing, to stand outside of himself in the clearing. This is the changed meaning of ex-sistence, which was already anticipated in the lecture on truth. Man is, in addition, a being who is charged with the task of *guarding* the clearing, an idea with which the essay on the work of art has made us familiar. Man is used by the clearing—as its "trustee."

The human character of man is put to the test, authenticated, in this task, which he has to perform by way of thinking. It is disavowed to the extent that man does not see it as a task. As it is stated at the beginning of the letter, "Thought brings to fulfillment the relation of Being to the essence of man" (p. 271). To fulfill is conceived as "to unfold something in the fullness of its essence" (p. 270). What is to be realized in thinking is the experiencing of the clearing and sustaining and articulating this experience in language. When this happens, "Language is the house of Being" (p. 270), hence the place where the clearing expressly makes its appearance, whereas ordinarily it is itself overlooked in favor of the entities that are cleared, presented, in this clearing. Its "stepping-into-appearance" is much more difficult to grasp than the appearing of entities, as they are understood from time to time, for it is itself never an entity, but is rather that which renders possible every experience of entities.

The task of thinking is to help the clearing find utterance, to guard the clearing, to make it accessible in its nature. It is this idea that has moved Heidegger from the beginning of his inquiry into Being and into *aletheia*.

How is the clearing related to Being? The clearing is Being, insofar as it becomes at all accessible to us. That is why Heidegger can say, "Thought . . . lets itself be called into service by Being in order to speak the truth of Being. It is thought which accomplishes this letting (*Lassen*)" (p. 271). For, the truth of Being is the clearing which has come to pass, forming the basis of all our bonds with beings and sustaining these bonds. We are herewith placed within the change that has occurred in the meaning of truth, so that truth no longer concerns the determination of entities, applies to beings or is something which corresponds with entities, but now means unconcealedness in the sense of the clearing, for it is as clearing that Being itself is conceived.

Being, clearing, truth of Being, *aletheia* are the same, and it is important that we think them in their selfsameness. The relation of Being to the nature of man as ek-sistence (ex-sistence) is to be understood now in the sense that "Being itself is the relationship" (p. 282). The place where the truth of Being finds expression, where it, so to speak, installs itself, is *Da-sein*, ex-sistence. "The standing in the clearing of Being I call the ex-sistence of man. Only man has this way to be. Ex-sistence, so understood, is not only the basis of the possibility of reason, *ratio*, but ex-sistence is that, wherein the essence of man preserves the source that determines him" (p. 277).

Ek-sistence is thus not understood here in the existentialistic sense, as man's efforts concerning his selfhood, by projecting himself on possibilities. Ek-sistence is conceived, rather, as standing out in the clearing, regarded as openness, which is not created or caused by man and which yet constitutes the basis of all creating and bringing about.

The entire "Letter on 'Humanism'" revolves round the ek-sistence of man, that is to say, round the attempt to understand man not as one living being among others but as the being who is distinguished by his relationship with Being. Heidegger's aim is to throw open for us the only realm in which a determination of the essential nature of man is possible. In this manner, man now is in fact invested with a dignity which surpasses every form of humanism, in so far as the latter puts man in the center. Here, the humanity of man is viewed in terms of "the nearness to Being" (p. 289), and his thinking as thinking of the openness as it occurs historically, that is, of the truth of Being. About this thinking, Heidegger says, "Thought acts in that it thinks. This is presumably the simplest and, at the same time, the highest form of action: it concerns man's relation to what is" (p. 271). Language and Being belong together because in language what finds utterance is the way Being itself is experienced. In thinking and poetizing, what is at issue each time is the primordial openness (compare Chapter 9). But we are so much under the spell of the technical interpretation of thought that we fail to catch sight of the dimension into which Heidegger wants to introduce us. Logic, according to Heidegger, is nothing but "the sanctioning of this interpretation which began with the Sophists and Plato" (p. 272).

This demolishes the prevailing view according to which we must turn to logic if we want to know what thinking means. What logic can teach us is only a specifically metaphysical interpretation of thought, only the technical interpretation or, as we may also call it, the instrumental interpretation of thought. But the meaning of "technology" includes more than this (compare Chapter 8).

"When thought comes to an end, expiring because it abandons its element, it replaces this loss by securing acceptance for itself as τέχνη, as an educational instrument and therefore as a scholarly enterprise and later as a cultural pursuit. Philosophy becomes progressively a technique of explanation in terms of ultimate cause" (p. 273).

As opposed to this, Heidegger attempts a kind of thinking which has Being for the element in which it moves. Element here should be conceived not as a neutral medium but as that from which thinking receives its strength. "It is the element which is the really potent thing [Vermögende], the ability, the power [Vermögen, faculty]. It takes care of thought and thus brings it into its essence. Thinking is the thinking of Being. The genitive has a double meaning. Thought is of Being insofar as thought, eventuated by Being, belongs to Being. Thought is at the same time thought of Being inasmuch as thought, belonging to Being, listens to Being" (p. 272). To think the clearing (Lichtung) in its way of clearing (Lichten) at any time is what listening to Being means for Heidegger.

Our position is no longer one in which man is understood as a subject, a subject which then projects various possible interpretations of what is. Rather, we are in the entirely different dimension which seeks to approach and comprehend the nature of man in terms of Being, that is, through the relationship of man to Being. We are no longer in the realm of metaphysics, which, indeed, thinks of the Being of beings, in the sense of being-ness, but "does not discriminate between the two" (p. 276). "Metaphysics does not ask for the truth of Being itself. Nor does it even ask, therefore, in what way the essence of man belongs to the truth of Being" (p. 276). Thinking of Being as that nearness or closeness within which we stand, which lets entities come close to us and upon which even our relation to ourselves is based—that is the meaning of the clearing, which must always be presupposed in order that we may be able to encounter entities. It should be evident that with this we have not arrived at the end point of a knowing process, that our quest has not culminated in some definitive knowledge. We are, on the contrary, at the beginning of a task, that of thinking of the nature of man in the context of the clearing happening at the time being. To mention only one difficulty, how is the change in the clearing to be conceived? Heidegger calls it destiny (*Geschick*, sending on a way, "mittence"), for man cannot bring it about but has rather to endure it. But, if so much depends on leading men to give express thought to the clearing, and if metaphysics is characterized as the epoch of the oblivion of Being, then the question arises whether there is not involved here, nevertheless, an essential contribution on the part of man also.

How are the question about Being and the question about truth related in this essay—which also means in this period of thinking? They coincide. Truth as unconcealedness is the clearing in the sense of truth of Being, that is, as Being. Truth of Being concerns the mode in which Being has revealed itself as the clearing, the clearing which man is called upon to guard, for on this rest his dignity and his distinction. "The occurrence of history [*Geschichte*] lives as the destiny of the truth of Being, and derives from it" (p. 284). This statement shows in what manner Heidegger thinks of truth, Being and historicity in their interconnectedness.*

* On this, see the interpretation of Heraclitus in the essay *"Aletheia"* in *Vorträge und Aufsätze* (Pfullingen: Neske, 1954, pp. 257–82), which was written in 1943 for the lecture course on Heraclitus and was published in 1954. Heraclitus is regarded here as the thinker who meditates on the idea of the clearing. The basic terms of Heraclitus mark the happening of the clearing.

8

Aletheia and the Nature of Technology ("The Question concerning Technology," 1953)

According to one current view, the Heidegger of *Being and Time* is closely associated with phenomenology, for which reason this work is especially valued, whereas the later Heidegger drifts away into poetizing thought-constructs which have nothing in common with the stringent ways of phenomenology and therefore no longer deserve to be taken into consideration.

Nothing could be more incorrect than such an apparently plausible classification. The later Heidegger is no less phenomenological than the early Heidegger. It is simply that what he now brings before his inquiring gaze surpasses what we usually identify as phenomenology. The very title of the lecture series given at the Bremen Club is evidence of their phenomenological stance: Insight into That Which Is (*Einblick in das, was ist*). Can there be a more phenomenological task than the one formulated here?

Of the four lectures, "Das Ding," "Das Ge-stell," "Die Gefahr" and "Die Kehre," let us discuss here the second. Its text was revised again and delivered on 18 November 1955 as a lecture entitled "The Question concerning Technology" ("Die Frage nach der Technik") at the conference The Arts in the Age of Technology, which was organized by the Bavarian Academy of Fine Arts.*

---

* Unless otherwise mentioned, page references in this chapter are to *Vorträge und Aufsätze* (Pfullingen: Neske, 1954). The text of this essay, with the last lecture, "Die Kehre," has also appeared in *Opuscula* 1 (Pfullingen: Neske, 1962).

The question is formulated with precision at the very beginning—at issue is the essence, the nature, of technology. ". . . The
essence of technology" is "not at all something technical" (p. 13),
just as the essence of the tree "is not itself a tree, which can be
found among the other trees" (p. 13).

The starting point is provided by the common conception of
technology as an instrument. In the course of the presentation this
conception is completely demolished.

We are in the curious situation that a means in the service of
the task of mastery must itself be brought under mastery because
it "threatens to escape from the control of man" (p. 15).

Now, Heidegger admits that this concept of technology as
instrument is "dreadfully correct" (p. 14), but he also draws a
distinction between the correct, or right, and the true, indicating
thus the course of thought which is intended to advance from representing the right to the apprehension of the true.

In order to be able to traverse this path leading from the right
to the true, we must have a clear idea of what we have called the
instrumental. It is a means. A means becomes a means by what it
brings about, what we are able to do with it. This leads to the
question of causality. Tradition speaks of the four causes: *causa
materialis* (matter), *causa formalis* (form), *causa efficiens* (efficient
cause) and *causa finalis* (final cause). In doing so, it appeals to the
authority of Aristotle. Heidegger now reminds us that in Greek
thought causality has nothing to do with effectuating and causing,
and that αἰτία means involving in debt or being responsible for
(*Verschulden*, being that to which something is owed or becomes
due). These four kinds of cause are four ways of being responsible
for. As an example, in the case of an offering cup, the silver, as the
matter, or ὕλη, is partly responsible for it, and so is the aspect, the
look or εἶδος. The offering cup belongs to the temple, the cult; this
is what really defines it, in which its purpose is consummated, the
τέλος. Lastly, the silversmith is jointly responsible for the fact that
this offering vessel is there, but not simply as one who has fabricated
it and produced it. "The silversmith is jointly responsible as being
that from where the putting forth and the resting-in-itself of the
offering cup derive and keep their initial emergence. The three

modes of responsibility mentioned before owe it to the deliberation of the silversmith that, and how, they make their appearance and come into play in the bringing forth of the offering cup" (p. 17). The *causa efficiens*, the cause most obvious to us, is not found at all in Aristotle in this form.

What is owed in this being-responsible-for, this involving in debt? It is "the lying there and lying ready of the silver cup as an offering-vessel" (p. 18). Through this being-responsible-for, the offering cup is able to appear, becomes present. To put it differently, it is the being-responsible-for that brings it about that "something not yet present (attains) presence" (p. 18). This occasioning in the sense of bringing forth is called by the Greeks ποίησις.

But *poiesis* is by no means limited to the agency of man. *Physis* (Nature), too, is *poiesis*. Constantly, by itself, Nature brings things into presence, lets entities be present—we need only think of the process of growing and ripening. Nevertheless, there is a difference between a bringing forth by man and natural production. The latter does not need any other agency to let something become present. The offering cup, on the other hand, requires the silversmith in order to be there. Nature is by itself and in itself a bringing forth, a producing.

What is the main point about bringing forth? What happens here? "The bringing-forth-from [*Her-vor-bringen*] brings forth from hiddenness into unhiddenness. Bringing-forth-from occurs only insofar as what is hidden becomes something unhidden" (p. 19). With this, however, we are already in the realm of *aletheia*. What at first appeared to be strange, even irreconcilable—bringing technology into relation with *aletheia*—now shows itself, on the contrary, as inseparably linked. If we think of *aletheia* as disclosure, which makes something unhidden in the sense of letting something appear and of attaining presence, then we can see that what is produced in every bringing-forth is indeed a presence, whether it is a question of manufacturing a new appliance, building a wall, furnishing a dwelling-place, cultivating a new species of plant, or putting up a work of art. This is the most comprehensive definition, not in the sense of mere generality but in the sense that the nature of what is happening here is expressly kept in sight.

But what has technology to do with that? It can also be looked upon, no doubt, as a kind of bringing-forth—of what kind remains to be examined further. If we grant this, it follows that technology also belongs to the realm of *aletheia*, of unconcealedness (truth). This may sound very strange to us, for in considering technology we think only of utility, of the means of production, the modes of production, the specific technique, the efficacy, the profitability, perhaps also of the conditions of production. We are, in other words, so fascinated by the technological that we never come to the point of inquiring what really goes on in the realm of the technological, what is therefore intrinsic to the nature of technology.

In Greek thought—from which, as we know, the concept of *techne* derives—*techne* and *episteme* belong together. Both are modes of knowing, of being-versed-in. The connection between *techne* and *aletheia* is not arbitrarily construed by Heidegger. For that we have unequivocal evidence in Aristotle's *Nicomachean Ethics*, Book VI, Chapters 3 and 4, where *techne* and *episteme* are explicitly regarded as modes of disclosing, of ἀληθεύειν. This text, as has been mentioned, was discovered early by Heidegger and stimulated his thinking; it is one of the germinative sources, so to speak, of his own thinking. Aristotle, moreover, already viewed *techne* with specific regard to the fact that here we are concerned with the disclosure or laying bare of something "which does not bring itself forth and is not yet there, which, therefore, can appear and turn out, now one way, now another" (p. 21). In this process, what is decisive is not making, manipulating, dealing-with, but the anticipation of the result that is to be achieved, of the house, for example, or the ship, the scaffolding and so on—what is decisive is the prevision of the figure or form to be attained. It is in this previsioning that there occurs the disclosure, which then constitutes the basis of everything that follows, from the procurement of materials and the rounds of work to the utilization of what has been brought forth. These are terms taken from modern ways of thinking, and they are intended to explain only how all this is at the service of previsioning the figure that is to be brought forth. For that, it is immaterial whether that which is to be brought forth is something already known, for example, a ship, or something novel in this respect, like a work of art.

Heidegger takes up a possible objection that, though this manner of defining *techne* may be applicable in the Greek sphere, it cannot be applied to the modern technology of power engines in its relation to modern science. Two questions arise. First, does the interconnectedness of *aletheia* and *techne* apply also to modern technology? And second, what is the intrinsic and essential nature of modern technology?

Heidegger's answer to the first question is yes. Even modern technology must be seen in the context of hiddenness and disclosure, and to be able to do so adequately one must analyze the second question. This is the central question of the essay on technology, for it concerns the manner in which, in modern technology, a disclosing or uncovering takes place. In other words, how do entities manifest themselves, appear, in the technological way of dealing with them? And this immediately leads to another question: How does the human being who is determined by technology respond to what is given, what kind of relation does he have to it?

The answer, which sounds harmless at first, is: In the technological attitude, everything is presented merely in respect to, or with a view to, its availability and disposability—everything becomes a *fund* (*Bestand*, stock or supply). As it is expressed in the unpublished first version, "the stock is something extant. It is extant insofar as it is on order or can be so [*auf ein Bestellen gestellt*]. Thus turned into something on order, as something disposable, it is put into use. Utilizing puts everything, from the very first, in such a position that what is thus placed follows the result that is to ensue. So placed, everything is: in consequence of . . . But the consequence [*Folge*] is something that has been from the very first intended as the desired result [*Erfolg*]. The result is that kind of consequence which itself remains geared to [*abgestellt*] the upshot of further consequences. The stock is sustained by a peculiar kind of placing or positing. We call it dis-posing [*Be-stellen*, positing in the manner of making disposable]." This becoming-a-fund of what is (beings) defines a new epoch. This was preceded by the epoch in which entities became *objects* and were apprehended as objects.

So long as that which is vis à vis man was and is an object (this first happened in the modern period with the determination of man as subject, for whom that which faces him is the object), a certain independence was still granted to it. I say "certain," because by becoming a subject, man regards himself, at least from the point of view of "knowing," as the really underlying foundation. In modern technology, this attitude is carried to an extreme. Not the cognitive but the conative, not that which pertains to knowing but that which pertains to doing, comes to the front, as I would put it. Obviously, doing is possible only through knowing, but here knowing is expressly judged in terms of what can be done with it. Doing, the ability to do, becomes the criterion of knowing. Such ability-to is then understood more and more in the sense of having-mastery-over, and the mastery has to show itself directly in the power of having something at one's disposal. This takes place in the *Bestand*, in the transformation of things into *stock*.

From this abbreviated account, it is true, one may get the impression that this change of the given from object to stock is simply a matter involving human caprice. This change may even be understood as a kind of reproach, so that we might then go on simply to include Heidegger among the opponents of technology and rest content with such inclusion. For we know, of course, that technology has its supporters and its opponents, and if we can assign someone to a class in this manner he is then neutralized basically by being thus pinned down, and no longer makes us uneasy. We now know ostensibly what the main point about this philosopher is. And if we then add to this description the term "irrationalism," in order really to scare away the reader but at the same time to produce the impression that we have discharged our duty as critical philosophers, the final judgment seems to have been pronounced irrevocably. This procedure fails, to be sure, when we take the trouble to read the text itself. For then we have to account for the fact that here it is not a question of glorifying or demonizing technology, but of understanding a state of affairs, in the very midst of which we stand and to which we are exposed, without yet properly understanding it. Heidegger's explanation is an attempt to arrive at such an understanding, an attempt that certainly takes us further than other interpretations of technology. To regard it as the only possible one is something he himself would disallow.

What matters here is not to acknowledge someone's authority; what does matter is at last to ask in what condition twentieth-century man exists. To preserve one's freedom, to set in motion a questioning that renders our own selves open to question—that is what matters. Nothing is easier than to be intoxicated by the triumphs of technology or simply to condemn technology by pointing out its negative aspects. In Heidegger's inquiry into the nature of technology, what happens is something different, namely, the attempt to give to technology the status that is due to it. In what manner this takes place and what that status is has to be shown in what follows.

We started from the fact that it is a mistake to think that the change in our attitude toward entities, the change from *object* to *stock* is due to human caprice. For, in this change we become aware of a transformation of unconcealedness (*aletheia*), a transformation which, according to Heidegger, is totally outside man's control, although it concerns him in his very depths. Such a transformation of unconcealedness is what we find in our dealings with entities in the manner of the Greek concept of *bringing-forth*, or in the *objectification* which occurred subsequently or, finally, in the contemporary mode of *turning into a fixed stock*.

"In pursuing technology, man participates in dis-posing as a mode of uncovering. Only, unconcealedness itself, within which the dis-posing exhibits itself, is never man's handiwork, as little so as that realm which man already traverses whenever, as a subject, he relates himself to an object" (p. 26).

We have seen that the nature of man is defined and sustained by his relationship to unconcealedness (compare Chapters 4, 5 and 6). The openness, which lets every manifest entity be encountered, is this unconcealedness. Along with the mode of openness, in which man is placed, his relation and approach to the manifest entities also changes. "Wherever man opens his eyes and ears, unlocks his heart, freely gives himself to his aspirations, his creativity and deeds, his praying and thanking, everywhere he finds himself within the unconcealed. Each time it calls man forth into the ways of uncovering meted out to him, its unconcealedness has already come to pass. When man, in his way, uncovers or discloses what is present within unconcealedness, he only answers to the address of unconcealedness" (p. 26).

The technological way of dealing with entities is thus not an activity arbitrarily chosen by man; rather, man is placed within, challenged into, this way of dealing with them by that specific mode of unconcealment itself which Heidegger calls the "framework" (Ge-stell).* How are we to understand this word? Heidegger takes it in an unaccustomed sense, because this entire course of thought is intended to lead us into the unaccustomed. The word "framework" makes us think of something thinglike because all our thinking (ideating, representing) welcomes having a foothold on what is thingly. What is thingly is visible, tangible, describable; it can be produced, used up and thrown away; with it, we know where we are. In order to have a sense of fixity in our residence, we fill the space within it with familiar things. To be sure, this is not the kind of consideration which concerns us here. Our concern here is with the openness in which we stand and through which that which is made manifest (being) becomes accessible—with the question, therefore, about unconcealedness, aletheia.

Ge-stell, the framework, is not of the nature of a thing but names a specific mode of unconcealedness. Which mode is that? That in which man is challenged "to disclose or uncover, in the manner of dis-posing, the real as stock. Ge-stell means the mode of disclosure which has its sway in the very nature of modern technology and is not itself anything technological" (p. 28).

It might be objected that one time we bring Ge-stell together with unhiddenness, another time, with disclosing. Is this not an inexact or at least a lax way of speaking? But, according to Heidegger, man's behavior or stance, that of disclosing—which we may call his basic activity, as different from his specific modes of behavior—is always based on and determined by the kind of unconcealedness prevailing at any time. And this unconcealedness becomes accessible to us by way of man's mode of acting, of relating himself, at the time. That unconcealedness prevailed in a different

---

* The dictionary defines Gestell as stage, frame, framework, skeleton. Ge-stell is coined on the model of Ge-setz (law, what is laid down, from setzen) and is meant to suggest the relationship of mutual placing (Stellen) in which man and thing challenge (stellen) each other (Tr.).

way in Greek times from the way it does at present is something that we cannot speculatively deduce or construct but can only gather from the Greeks' way of dealing with and understanding that which is and from their own self-understanding. There is an interplay between unhiddenness and disclosure (*Entbergung*); they constitute a unitary phenomenon, and it is important that we interpret them historically. The distinction made among different ways of dealing, having relationships, with things—bringing-forth, objectifying and dis-posing—are differences of unconcealedness, and this means, at the same time, of disclosing.

The fact that machinery of various sorts (the words for which, in German, are often formed like *Gestell*) is bound up with the operations and organization of technology, should not lead us to think of *Gestell* as referring to what is of such thingly character. Heidegger wants, rather, to inquire back into the unconcealedness peculiar to technology. This gives a clear indication of the status which Heidegger accords to technology and shows how far removed his account is from every description of technology as an instrument.

Heidegger expressly points out that the word *Stellen* in *Gestell* is intended to keep alive the connection with *Stellen* in the sense of bringing forth or producing, as it occurs in *poiesis*. In the kind of producing that conforms to *poiesis*, entities are brought into presence, although not in such fashion that they are now there like a fund, or stock, at our disposal but in such a way that, in this putting, something makes its appearance.

The Greek letting-become-present that we have in this bringing-forth in the sense of *poiesis* and the modern securing of resources as a challenging of Nature in the sense of the *Gestell* are, so to speak, two opposite poles which, however, belong—and this must not be overlooked—in the same dimension, namely, the basic dimension of unhiddenness (*aletheia*). Unhiddenness happens in both, though in very different ways. In his Bremen lecture series *Einblick in das, was ist*, Heidegger has brought out how modern science is in essence technological. This means that what goes on in modern science corresponds to the truth of Being in the sense of *Gestell*, that this truth finds utterance in it.

Here we cannot pursue further the question of how, in

modern science, even before the development of technology, there is at work the tendency to challenge Nature in the sense of exhibiting an interrelationship of forces which can be calculated beforehand. "The modern physical theory of Nature prepared the way not primarily for technology but for the essence of technology. For, the gathering together [*Versammeln*], the *logos*, which challenges men to a disposing uncovering already has its sway in physics" (p. 29). Modern physics is called "the herald, as yet unrecognized in respect of its origin, of the *Ge-stell*" (p. 29). Causality now is no longer a bringing about or occasioning which brings forth, in the sense of being-responsible-for, nor is it *causa efficiens* or *causa formalis*. Heidegger offers a hint: "Presumably, causality shrivels into a challenged announcing of simultaneously or succesively to be secured stocks" (pp. 30–31).

In a second step, the reflection is focused on grasping the *Ge-stell*. Just because in the *Ge-stell* there is meant the thought not of anything thingly but rather of a mode of man's relationality to entities, it is necessary to circumscribe more closely the thought it is meant to convey. When we speak of man's relationality the question immediately arises: How does this relationality come about? Can man simply develop relationships at his pleasure and then abolish them, thus distancing himself from them? Or is such developing governed by a dictate, a dictate which remains hidden from us in the first instance and mostly, which perhaps will remain so for a long time to come?

Heidegger deliberately avoids speaking of relationality (man as the center of relations) because ordinarily it is understood in the sense that the modern ego, which has at last found a way to justify its existence, is now in a position to develop itself according to its own plans and wishes, which means that it can put into play those relationships with entities which are agreeable to it. In other words, the ego as subject is now that which, properly speaking, is, and everything that is not of the nature of a subject receives its justification for being, its title to be recognized as a being, by the grace of the subject. Precisely in its modern form, this position has been exposed and seen through by Heidegger as a particular manner in which metaphysics has evolved. But, because we stand within this metaphysical tradition and are determined by, borne on, it, it is therefore very difficult for us to break loose from this mode of approach.

In the Ge-stell, there takes place a particular mode of disclosing. How does it occur? "Does this disclosing happen somewhere beyond all human doing? No. But it also does not happen only *in* man and not definitely and in any important way, *through him*" (p. 31). Man is thus involved in it but he is, nevertheless, not the master of disclosing or, as we may also put it, of the openness into which all our acts and attitudes are embedded.

This answer is of a more negative than positive character. But this is not by chance, nor is it a rhetorical dodge meant to heighten the tension of the reader. It is, on the contrary, an indication that here we have left behind us the objective realm with its unequivocal questions and answers. This, however, does not at all mean that we now enter a realm in which all cows are grey, but rather that here a change in the manner of thinking is required which is not easy to accomplish. That is why Heidegger takes up once again what has to be thought in the Ge-stell: "The Gestell is the gathering [agent] in that placing [Stellen] which challenges [stellt] man to disclose, in the manner of dis-posing, the real as a stock. As thus challenged, man stands within the realm in which the Ge-stell has its sway" (p. 31).

We do not know how it could come to this, but we know quite well what is happening in consequence of what has thus come about. In the Ge-stell we experience a particular mode of disclosing; we are placed in it as a kind of destiny. To ponder this destiny expressly is one of man's fundamental tasks, according to Heidegger. Why? Because by such pondering a pre-eminent possibility opens up, namely, the possibility of not simply remaining restricted to this particular way of dealing with what is (in the sense of dis-posing) but of being able to inquire back how such a thing as unhiddenness is involved in it.

"Because this [destiny] brings man, from time to time, on a way of disclosing, man incessantly goes, thus on the way, to the very limits of the possibility of following and cultivating what has been disclosed through the dis-posing and of deriving all criteria from it. As a result of this, the other possibility is closed, that man may, preferably and more and ever more originally, yield to the nature of the unconcealed and its unconcealedness, so that he may experience the belongingness to disclosing, be made use of by it, as his own essence or nature" (pp. 33–34).

While it seemed first as if there was no possibility of escaping from a particular relationality, or mode of being related—in this case, that of dis-posing—the text quoted above states that there is indeed another possibility opened up in and by thinking. It lies in inquiring into the dimension that is the primary basis of every kind of disclosing, the dimension of unconcealedness. This quest, the text further says, enables man to find himself, that is, to reach a determination of his own true nature or being, which is sustained by the relationship to unconcealedness (compare the "Letter on 'Humanism'"). For, there can be such a thing as unconcealedness only for a being who is himself open and who can, standing thus within the unconcealed, bear and carry through this unconcealedness.

This standing-in-the-unhidden and carrying-out-the-unhiddenness does not at all mean that man is a mere bearer or messenger, one who merely carries out, puts into effect. How unconcealment comes about does not, of course, rest with him. But, on the other hand, man need not necessarily be totally absorbed in dis-posing, for he is capable of recollecting that which delivers such a thing as dis-posing at all. Once again we come up against the difficulty that we tend to represent unconcealedness as an empty medium which receives entities into itself. But there is more at stake here, as should have been evident from the very variety of modes of disclosure mentioned above: disclosing as *poiesis*, in the sense of bringing-forth; disclosing as objectification; disclosing as dis-posing. Each time, what is appears in a different manner, and man also understands himself differently.

Precisely in the case of dis-posing we find how man himself is allowed to be only something dis-posable—and yet, he puts on airs of being absolute master over every being, as if by doing so he could outmaneuver the loss he has sustained. Man seems everywhere to encounter only himself.[17] In Heidegger's interpretation, however, the very opposite becomes evident. "All the same, it is precisely nowhere that man, in truth, encounters now his own self, that is, himself in his nature or being" (p. 35).

How can such a thing be maintained, in view of the undoubted fact that the effectiveness and action of man are taking on such proportions that we suddenly find ourselves in the unforeseen predicament of making our environment progressively uninhabitable? Do we not constantly come up against man's action even where we do not want it, in Nature as our environment? Is man not omnipresent?

But then, what Heidegger maintained was, not that man does not constantly make himself noticeable, seeking to have everything in his grip, but that the essential nature of man eludes him, that we do not come upon this essence. We must recall that it is just this essence which Heidegger thinks of in terms of the relationship of man to unconcealment, that this relationship, which we called the fundamental relationship, is the basic, governing element. And it is this relationship which, in fact, cannot be seen when the dis-posing attitude is consistently adopted. So little of it is visible that a thinking which starts out from this relationship and brings everything into relation with it, is bound to be discredited as talking about nonexistent things. After all, we ourselves, as soon as we mention unconcealedness, are in this difficult position of not being able to produce for inspection anything palpable, at which one may grasp or from which one may even draw comfort. To put it differently, we find it an extremely odd interpretation of man when Heidegger speaks of the relationship to unconcealedness as the essential nature of man and when man is conceived as one who exists, as one who stands out in unconcealedness, taking charge of unconcealedness and preserving it. Had he been speaking of man in terms of a being producing itself by means of work, we would have at once understood what was meant. But here, nothing whatever is produced—even the unconcealedness must not be regarded as a product of human action or as something accomplished by man.

That in the course of the history of metaphysics a change in the interpretation of what is takes place is something we can see easily for ourselves; it can be proved by textual evidence, once we have understood and accepted the basic principle of interpretation employed by Heidegger. But when it comes to the step, which for him is the main thing, of inquiring back into the happening which lies hidden beneath this history as its basis, we refuse to go along, we lightly come up with the insinuation that, after all, this is only a sort of postmetaphysical speculation. We should not adopt such an attitude, as though Heidegger's procedure were something obvious. It is something totally unusual. Heidegger himself by no means saw and conceived this thought in this way from the very beginning. It is not as if he began by setting it up as his thesis, trying subsequently to provide documentary evidence for it; on the contrary, he has arrived at this insight step by step. We have attempted to show how he started out very early from the thought of *aletheia*, but it was a good while, decades, before, questing and thinking, he was able to express it in the way this was done in *Einblick in das, was ist.*

With the supremacy of the *Ge-stell*, according to Heidegger, the threat has become actual "that it might be denied to man to enter into a more primordial mode of disclosing and thus to experience the call of a more originative truth" (p. 36). This is because truth is not located in the statement, in the true sentence, but is, rather, as unhiddenness, that destiny within which man stands, which he has to bear and carry out, depending upon how he is able to experience that which is. That is why it is possible for Heidegger to think of unconcealedness as that which vouchsafes. It grants the openness in which man is historically situated and which makes entities accessible to him in determinate ways.

We are trying to understand what it is that constitutes the ambiguous character of the essence of technology. So far, we have merely referred to the characteristic feature of the highest peril, the fact that man is so completely sucked up in the frenzy of disposing that the relationship to truth as disclosure is totally blocked and that other possibilities of disclosing cannot also be seized as possibilities. This is only one side of the matter. If in the *Ge-stell* a certain mode of unhiddenness is exhibited, if in every kind of unhiddenness something like a granting is involved, then precisely here, too, this idea of something that grants may become a matter calling for thought. Thus man may be conceived in terms of his relationship to truth, which is Heidegger's constant endeavor. Such thinking may contribute something toward surmounting the loss of substance which results from the sheer dis-posing and securing of resources. This could then become the start of a process of trans-formation—a transformation possible in the sense of a happening that rescues, which can emerge suddenly in the midst of utmost peril. It is quite conceivable that such a transformation may come about precisely from the side of art, for in art the main point has for long been a letting-come-to-light of that which is, and that means also of man himself. It may also come about precisely in thinking, as Heidegger understands it, as distinguished from philos-ophizing (compare Chapter 9). In thinking, that which is to be thought, the matter of thought, is unconcealedness itself as well as the disclosure and concealment occurring in it. That is why the thinkers who have been the first to reflect on it, whom Heidegger calls the early thinkers—Anaximander, Parmenides, Heraclitus—have been the ones to whose interpretative appropriation he has devoted himself for years.

In attempting to understand these trains of thought, the ques-tion which obtrudes itself and demands our attention with ever-greater urgency, is this: How could the kind of unhiddenness meant by the Ge-stell possibly come about? Heidegger's answer is that it is Being itself which shows itself in this manner. In the as yet un-published lecture "Die Gefahr" ("The Peril"), he has expressly reflected upon the interconnection of *physis* and *thesis* and shown how in the bringing-forth of *physis* a positing (*Stellen*) is also in-volved. Entities are brought out from hiddenness into unhiddenness and thus become present. These present entities can be transformed by human positing or setting up, for example, a stone wall. Positing in this sense is *thesis*, a setting-forth, as conceived in the Greek manner. This presupposes that unconcealedness is somehow ex-perienced already, for it is only in the realm of unconcealedness that any setting-forth or producing is possible. In the letting-become-present of entities in the manner of *physis*, Heidegger sees the essential origin of the subsequent positing in the manner of the *Gestell*. We should not, of course, lose sight of the difference between the positing of *physis* and the positing of this *Gestell* if we are to grasp the extent of the change from the Greek manner of experiencing entities as what is present to the present-day experience of beings as a stock. That we may at last come to the point of seeing this change at all, of reflecting on it, of recognizing it as our history, that is Heidegger's purpose.

In conclusion, we may refer to a difficulty inherent in this interpretation. This is the difficulty of sketching the position occupied by man. On the one hand, he is a being who is used by unconcealedness. It is destiny that "first conveys to man that share in disclosing which the happening of disclosure needs. As one who is thus needed and used, man is under the ownership of the event of truth" (p. 40). On the other hand, man is also required to make a contribution of his own, by way of thinking or in the manner of artistic production. Perhaps there are also other modes; formerly, Heidegger considered the activity of establishing a state also as one such mode. It is not easy to understand how such a position is to be conceived, because from the perspective of our ordinary conceptual world we tend to think of it in either a passive or an active sense, hence concluding either that man is delivered up to destiny or that he determines it. Heidegger, however, accepts neither alternative. Man must be open to the call of destiny, but he is not a slave to it. This is the only way one can think of the possibility that man may be extricated once again from his ominous destiny, may be delivered from it. That is a deliverance which can ensue if we follow the path of questing for the primordial—hence that going back, mentioned above, to the first thinkers, for whom unconcealedness was the momentous, inspiring event.

9

Poetry—Thinking—Language
("The Nature of Language," 1957)

The further we advance in our reading of Heidegger, the more evident is our difficulty in discussing his thinking. It is therefore necessary that we confront this specific difficulty.

Two possibilities are open to us. We can either view this thinking from the outside and seek to analyze and criticize it, or we can endeavor to understand it from within.

In regard to the first possibility, it is not at all difficult to nail Heidegger's position down to particular statements, to reduce his thinking to particular theses and then to maintain that these are untenable, because they do not answer to one's own manner of questioning. If our aim is to judge Heidegger in terms of traditional conceptual schemata, this is the obvious way to proceed. Soon, however, it turns out that this just will not do. What does this mean? It can mean either that Heidegger's position is untenable or that this procedure is inappropriate. The interpreter naturally tries to adopt the first alternative, for otherwise he would be obliged to give up and abandon his interpretation. The underlying difficulty, however, is of a more fundamental character. When a thinker like Heidegger seeks, by way of thinking the tradition through, to lay open its happening and at the same time to see through its limited character, he must also gradually abandon the language of this tradition. This can be seen quite clearly in Heidegger's case. Thus, in *Being and Time* there is no longer any place for the traditional subject-object set of problems, for a new manner of understanding man is inaugurated with the concept of Dasein. However, we still find traces of the traditional conceptual apparatus, as in the application of the concepts of ontology and transcendence. The retrospective inquiry into the ground which we meet with for such an extended period in Heidegger's thinking, is also finally left behind in the last works, recognized as a legacy, so to speak, of metaphysics and is overcome. These comments are meant only to make it clear how the language of thinking also changes with the progression of thought. This change is not something to complain about but is evidence that this thinking is not frozen but remains on the move, that it is a quest which cannot be quieted. So long as the traditional language provides the level at which the interpretation is carried on, a live quest such as this is bound to be felt as a stumbling block. The interpreter resists what is demanded of him. He blames the thinker for the strain to which he is subjected. This leads to the most illuminating and also the most vacuous criticism, namely, that these difficulties prove that this thinking is on the wrong track.

We stand within the tradition of Western metaphysics, whether we are conscious of it or not, whether we attempt to understand this tradition from its origins or believe that we can dispense with it. We are so completely caught up in this tradition that we try, necessarily, to gain access to Heidegger in terms of that. And we then find it hard to see how he moves away from just this tradition and what such moving away means here. He does not thoughtlessly shake it off; he does not reject it but, on the contrary, remains engaged in a passionate dialogue with it. We can observe this in the published writings—especially in the great Nietzsche interpretation, which sees in Nietzsche the end of metaphysics and takes in its sweep philosophers from Plato to Nietzsche, including interpretations of Leibniz, Kant, Hegel and Schelling as well. If, instead of keeping in mind this wrestling with past thinkers, we translate Heidegger back into the language of metaphysics, the task of understanding seems to be lightened. In reality, however, it is rendered impossible, because what we then grasp is not what Heidegger thought, but rather that from which he distances himself. It is therefore not difficult to come up with criticisms—only, they are completely off the mark.

What can we say about the second possibility of interpretation? It tries to get into the Heideggerian position at one leap and hold itself firmly there, without, however, preparing for and executing the leap as a leap. Basically, one wishes to spare oneself the leap by acting as though one had always taken Heidegger's position. What has been stated by Heidegger is no longer translated into another language and alienated by doing so. But now another difficulty arises. One loses sight of the kind of arguing and wrestling that were required to arrive at this new way of seeing. A false impression is generated, as though Heidegger had one day simply jumped out of the tradition and then forcibly initiated something new, something novel but which at the same time presents the appearance of a relapse into the archaic, something novel that is in fact hostile to the new, the modern. In interpretations of this kind, one tends to limit oneself to reiterating in a minor key, as it were, what Heidegger has stated, so that the question at once arises: What is the sense of such a repetition? Is it not just a feeble imitation, in place of which we should rather have the original?

Then there is the question: Does the interpreter really speak from the attitude and point of view of Heidegger, or does he merely think that he is doing so? There is a certain presumptuousness in this way of talking. The interpreter poses as Heidegger, knows what this or that concept means and can spare himself, so to speak, the trouble of traveling for himself the toilsome path on which Heidegger had set out. Perhaps he even thinks that he knows better than Heidegger himself, whereas what he offers as an interpretation is nothing but a garbled repetition. He denies the movement inherent in Heidegger's manner of thinking, from the beginning to the present moment, and proceeds as if Heidegger's insights were due to bursts of sheer inspiration, whereas Heidegger himself repeatedly points to the necessity of the movement of thought that must be executed (compare "The Principle of Identity" in *Identity and Difference*)—indeed, he insists that his thinking be understood as a path.

If both possibilities of interpretation—the alienating interpretation from the "outside" and the interpretation based on a leap to the "inside"—are inappropriate, is there anything at all we can do? Admitting at the outset that we are not at all in a position to interpret—that is what we can do. An interpretation ought to open up vistas, reveal something; it should be capable of exhibiting what lies hidden in a thinking, what is its basis, which dimensions are opened up by it; it should be able to show the kind of transformation of understanding that such thinking has brought about. We cannot, today, do any of this, so far as Heidegger's thinking is concerned. To be sure, criticisms of his interpretations are brought forward and resentment is expressed against their forced, "violent" character. People seek either to unmask them or, contrariwise, to take delight in the unusual, try to feel edified by it. The early Heidegger is played off against the later. When all is said and done, however, all this remains irrelevant, passing by the event that is this thinking. Till today, we have not got to the point of having a dialogue with Heidegger because there is no one to conduct such a dialogue, and his thinking continues to strike us as strange and to amaze us.

What then can be the point of an attempt such as the present one? It is meant to try to lead the reader to Heidegger, to encourage him to read the original texts. We easily tend to adopt the prejudice that when something presents us with a difficulty, it is not the matter that is to blame but he who speaks about this matter. We may perhaps do well to attempt, for once, the opposite approach, to set out with the assumption that the difficulty lies in the matter itself—and perhaps also in the inertia that prevents us from acknowledging a difficulty.

The whole complex of problems regarding poetry, thinking and language needs to be pursued from its beginning in the discussion in *Being and Time*, then on through "The Origin of the Work of Art," "Hölderlin and the Essence of Poetry" (1936), the Hölderlin interpretations of "Homecoming/To His Relatives," "As on a Holiday . . .," "Remembrance," to the Trakl interpretations in *On the Way to Language*. That is not possible here. We confine ourselves to two texts from *On the Way to Language*— "The Nature of Language" and "Words."*

* Page references in this chapter are to *On the Way to Language*, translated by Peter D. Hertz and Joan Stambaugh (New York: Harper & Row, 1971).

The introduction to the three lectures, entitled "The Nature of Language," describes what is at issue as "undergoing an experience with language" (p. 57). This is not meant to suggest that we should carry out experiments with language but "that for once we turn our attention to *our relation to language*" (p. 58), that we recollect that language is our abode. We have to make up our minds about a matter that concerns our own being. It is not a question of accumulating knowledge about language, as in metalanguage or metalinguistic studies. At the very beginning, Heidegger makes it clear that his inquiry into the nature of language is not intended to be conducted on the lines of modern metaphysics any more, and the investigations of a metalinguistic character remain bound to just this track. "Metalinguistics is the metaphysics of the thoroughgoing technicalization of all languages into the sole operative instrument of interplanetary information" (p. 58).

In undergoing an experience with language our objective is that language itself may "bring itself to language," give utterance to itself. Language has the special peculiarity that we live in it, are at home in it, but usually without expressly turning our attention to it, hence without catching sight of what it is in itself. In order to extricate himself from this situation, Heidegger appeals to a poet. He does so because the poet not only possesses a privileged relationship to language but also gives utterance to this relationship. Just as Hölderlin has expressly sought to grasp the nature of the poet in his own poetry, so has Stefan George sought to grasp the relationship of the poet to language. That is why the central position in this discussion is occupied by an interpretation of George's poem "Words," which appeared in 1919 and was later included in the collection *Das Neue Reich*.

> Wonder or dream from distant land
> I carried to my country's strand
>
> And waited till the twilit norn
> Had found the name within her bourn—
>
> Then I could grasp it close and strong
> It blooms and shines now the front along . . .

Once I returned from happy sail
I had a prize so rich and frail,

She sought for long and tidings told:
"No like of this these depths enfold."

And straight it vanished from my hand,
The treasure never graced my land . . .

So I renounced and sadly see:
Where word breaks off no thing may be.

The first triad tells us about the power of the poet—he is able
to bring home marvelous things and treasures seen in dream. The
goddess of fate, Norn, presents him with names for what he has
brought in. Thus, that which already is, is made to shine forth by
the word, even for others. It is through the name that the poet
keeps hold of his vision, which is then able to unfold itself by
virtue of this retention. What is presented here is a high point of
the poetic act. The triad culminates in the evocation of a presence.
"It blooms and shines now the front along . . . ," exhibiting the
stabilization and rendering-present that occurs in this part of the
poem, in which names are accorded sovereignty over things.

In contrast to this, the second triad speaks of an experience in
which the poet brings for the purpose of being given a name, not
a faraway thing but something obvious—he calls it a jewel, a
treasure. We may here conjecture that it is *the* jewel which makes
the being of its bearer manifest—enables this being itself to appear. But precisely for that the goddess Norn cannot find any
name. Since she had found, till then, a name for every entity, it
might be supposed that what is now presented is a nonentity. But,
on the other hand, it is called a jewel all the same, specially
precious, and an entity therefore of a superlative kind.

With the absence of the word for it, the treasure disappears,
the poet cannot retain it. Here a new mode of the word's being
appears. The word can provide a name not merely for something
that already is, "it is no longer just a name-giving grasp reaching

for what is present and already represented" (p. 146), but it is, on the contrary, that which bestows presence as well.

The poem ends with the verse:

So I renounced and sadly see:
Where word breaks off no thing may be.

How are we to understand this conclusion? It mentions, according to Heidegger, not that which is to be renounced but the realm into which renunciation must enter. "What the poet learned to renounce is his formerly cherished view regarding the relation of thing and word" (p. 65). The "may be" should be understood as an imperative; or, to put it more precisely, in the relinquishment of his previous understanding there is also contained a command. "The word avows itself to the poet as that which holds and sustains a thing in its being" (pp. 65–66).

The poet experiences himself as one who is entrusted with the word, who is its trustee. Here, expression is given to a boundary-experience for which no word is adequate, for which Norn cannot find a name. But this should not be taken in a purely negative sense. For with the learning of the renunciation, the potency of the word also becomes apparent. In the mood of sadness Heidegger discovers "the mood of releasement [Gelassenheit] into the nearness of what is withdrawn but at the same time held in reserve for an originary advent" (p. 66). We can characterize this mood as also the basic mood in Heidegger's thinking, as the mood of the "time of need." In the withdrawal of Being and in the thinking of this withdrawal, there is the announcement of a new advent, once the withdrawal as such has been experienced. This becomes clear in Heidegger's attitude toward metaphysics. He thinks of the history of metaphysics as the epoch of the oblivion of Being (Seinsvergessenheit). This epoch is not at once terminated with the emergence of Heidegger's thought, but the absence of Being is first expressly thought of and comprehended as the epoch of the remoteness of Being, providing thus the possibility of a reversal, about which no one·can say when it will come about. These comments on language, on the poet's word, are not just incidental problems which happen to engage Heidegger, but, in them, his basic experience is gathered together, and a chastened repetition of the question about Being occurs in them.

What matters to Heidegger here is listening to the promise of language. "Language must, in its own way, avow to us itself—its nature" (p. 76). Once this happens, we become capable of undergoing a thinking experience with language. The preparation for such an experience consists in having a glimpse of the neighborhood of poetry and thinking, in our ability to establish ourselves in this neighborhood.

Heidegger's interpretation is intended to show that in spite of the important statements about language we find made in the realm of thought, in spite of the exciting things that have been composed in language, the essence or being of language "nowhere brings itself to word as the language of being [Wesen]" (p. 81). We saw earlier that while we are speaking, language itself falls back, withdraws, in favor of what is said in it. This withdrawal might have its ground in "that language holds back its own origin and so denies its being to our usual notions [Vorstellen]" (p. 81). The difficulty here is in refraining from personifying at once such a state of affairs, which this formulation may tempt us to do. Heidegger offers a conjecture as to why the essential nature of language denies itself to us: " . . . the two kinds of utterance par excellence, poetry and thinking, have not been sought out in their proper habitat, their neighborhood" (p. 81). It is precisely this that Heidegger will do in the second of three lectures in the series The Nature of Language.

The attempt to interpret the concluding verse of George's poem "The Word" was intended to show that here the issue is the relationship between thing (entity) and word, that indeed it is the word that enables the thing (entity) to be and keeps it in being. The word hence does not merely stand in relation to the thing, but is "what holds and keeps the thing as thing" (p. 82 f.) and is what Heidegger calls the "relationship" (Verhältnis, literally a holding together), by which he does not simply mean a mere relation but something which holds and keeps, in the sense of that which vouchsafes, grants.

What poets and thinkers have in common is the element of
language, though we do not yet know how "element" is to be conceived and how it changes according to whether words are used
poetically or as in thinking. From the approach adopted in interpreting George's poem, it seemed that we had reached what
looked like the neighborhood of poetry and thinking, that what
was poetically composed could become accessible by approaching it
from the side of thinking. But as Heidegger now points out, something crucial is missing in this attempt, namely, a grasp of this
neighborhood *as such*, the neighborhood in quest of which the
interpretation started out. Whenever we speak we already dwell in
language, but expressly to come in sight of this sojourn is the most
difficult of tasks. And if it is this sojourn that defines man in his
very being, then, it may be added, returning "into the sphere of
human being" (p. 85) is what is presented as a task to us in the
dimension of thought that is Heidegger's and is what lies at the
basis of all his exertions and aspirations. The sphere mentioned
here must not, however, be understood in the sense of a "fixed
place" to which man is, as it were, pinned down but as the place at
which he is provided with his possibilities of development.

Heidegger never thinks of this return as an arbitrary reversion
to the archaic, which is impossible for the simple reason that
Dasein is conceived as historical and Being itself is thought of in
the dimension of time (compare "Time and Being" in *On Time
and Being*). In this context, it is true, Heidegger contrasts the
"step back into the location of man's being (nature)" with the
"progress into the machine world" (p. 85), where the latter is
evidently referred to in a critical sense. At the back of this, however, is the thought that so long as man does not know what his
nature is and in what it is grounded, every advance in the sense of
achieving technical mastery remains questionable. For here, he who
advances can measure his advance only in terms of his increasing
ability to gain mastery over Nature and has no need to know anything about his own plight or to find out whether the aspect of
Nature which becomes visible in this mode of dealing with it is
really Nature as such.

While interpreting the poem by George, Heidegger left as an

open question in what sense the jewel is to be understood. Now he offers a suggestion: The precious gem, for which the goddess is unable to find a word, is nothing but the word itself. This shows the limits of the poet. In the land of the poet, the word for the word cannot be found. Can this perhaps be achieved if we approach the matter from the side of thinking? The word is not a thing. So long as we look for it among things, we can never find it. The word *is* not, if we reserve the "is" for the realm of entities, and yet, it is in a more pre-eminent sense than all things. " . . . we may never say of the word that it is, but rather that it gives [*es gibt*] . . ." (p. 88).

It gives, not in the sense of being there, of being present on hand, as when one says, "This year there are (*es gibt*) fine apples," but in the sense of *giving*, a gift. By its very nature the word gives, bestows. What it confers is Being. This should not be understood, however, in the sense that the word generates the thing as, according to the medieval concept, God's thoughts originate all that is. We must call back to mind the concept of the clearing, in which all entities are able to appear without being themselves created by the clearing.

We are in search of the neighborhood of poetry and thinking and have so far arrived only at the point of seeing that it is out of language that their nearness can be grasped. "For man is man only because he is granted the promise of language, because he is needful to language, that he may speak it" (p. 90). This sentence gives expression to a crucial shift. Till now our concern was the determination of man's proper nature; in the process we came upon language as the abode of man, which as such remains hidden from man even though it is that which is closest to him. Now, man suddenly recedes into the background and language comes to the forefront. We are at the very opposite pole of the concept according to which language is merely a means of communication, an article of use, so to speak. It is man who appears here as the one used—by language. Is that not an impermissible hypostatization of language? In what way must we now understand language if it is language that is the essential thing and man only serves it?

In order to advance on this path of questioning, Heidegger

surmises the essential nature of language to lie in "saying." " 'To say,' related to the Old Norse 'sagan' means to show: to make appear, set free, that is, to offer and extend what we call World, lighting and concealing it" (p. 93). This may be, in the first place, a logical development of thought regarding language based on "The Origin of the Work of Art," in which letting-appear is perceived in its double character of releasing and holding back, of disclosure and concealment (compare *Poetry, Language, Thought,* p. 53).

The guiding principle for the experience of language is as follows: "The being [*Wesen*, essence] of language: the language of being [*Wesen*]" (p. 94). In this key statement a reversal is executed that, once we have grasped it and have ourselves undergone it, takes us to the very limit.

In the first sentence, essence (*Wesen*) is understood in the sense of the "what" (τὸ τί ἐστιν, what something is). Its subject is language and the point here is to understand the *essentia* of this subject. "Essence so understood becomes restricted to what is later called the concept, the idea or mental representation by means of which we propose to ourselves and grasp what a thing is" (p. 94). (This at the same time refers to the first triad of the poem "The Word," by Stefan George.) Essence as thus understood holds us fast within the realm of metaphysical representation.

In regard to the second sentence, it is imperative that we do not merely convert it, so that now the essence may be thought of as the subject and language as a predicate of it. This conversion is meant rather to bring about a transformation, a change from metaphysical *representing* to a no-longer-metaphysical *thinking*. We find this all the harder to accomplish, for we have been wholly nurtured in metaphysical representing and we have inherited from it our way of looking at things. Hence, this new mode of speaking is bound to appear strange to us.

Whereas in the first sentence being, that is, essence, means "whatness," in the second sentence it should be conceived as "lasting" and "lingering," though not simply in the sense of mere duration but as that which concerns, touches or affects us, moves us. ". . . language belongs to this persisting being, is proper to what moves [*Be-wegende*, that which opens up paths] all things because that is its most distinctive property" (p. 95). How are we to think of this all-moving, path-generating be-ing? In the later writings, Heidegger conceives it as the "fourfold" (compare "The Thing"), as the four world-regions of earth, sky, men (mortals) and divinities, which in their interplay constitute the world.

In his interpretation of verses from the fifth strophe of "Bread and Wine," Heidegger finds in Hölderlin the word as ". . . the region that determines earth and sky to be world regions, as it makes earth and sky, the streaming of the deep and the might of the heights, encounter one another" (p. 100). Thus, language is here understood as that on which the interplay of the four world-regions is based. It is in this interplay that *nearness* comes about. Nearness and saying as letting-appear constitute the essential mode of being of language—they are the same.

"Language, Saying of the world's fourfold, is no longer only such that we speaking human beings are related to it in the sense of a nexus existing between man and language. Language is, as world-moving Saying, the relation of all relations. It relates, maintains, proffers, and enriches the face-to-face encounter [*das Gegen-einander-über*] of the world's regions, holds and keeps them, in that it holds itself—Saying—in reserve" (p. 107).[18]

The sounding of language is not regarded here as a result of physiological and physical processes. "The sound of language . . . is held within the harmony that attunes the regions of the world's structure, playing them in chorus" (p. 101). Heidegger has here achieved a loftiness of utterance in regard to language with which we are unable to catch up, for which reason what he says is certain to astound us. Language is here regarded as that primordial reality which holds the world-regions together, which at the same time means, holds them apart. We are always in danger of slipping back into the customary ways of representing, of regarding language as something like an external bond, so that it is hard to see where this bond comes from and from where it derives its power to bind together.

If we understand Heidegger with some adequacy, we should be able to see that language is not a separate entity, to be found outside the fourfold of the world—where else can it be?—but is in the fourfold itself, as the relation of the fourfold. Language is not a transcendental power—to regard it so would be to conceive it metaphysically—but is the nearness that prevails in the fourfold, for which Heidegger suggests the term "nighness" (*Nahnis*). It is, in other words, the primordial gathering (*Versammlung*).

This is the point at which Heidegger meets Heraclitus and his idea of *Logos*, which Heidegger had interpreted decades earlier as the original gathering. Language as the primordial gathering is soundless. From it comes the gift of saying "is" to man. The gathering, soundless language of stillness is the language of essence, of Being, one might say, provided we do not represent it metaphysically. In the last verse of the poem by George cited earlier, Heidegger sees a poetic allusion to the breaking of the word, as it is familiar to us, and a suggestion for realizing through thinking the nature of language as stillness. That is possible only because poetry and thought meet as neighbors in language—that is, in nearness.

In conclusion, let us submit for consideration a thought from Heidegger's latest writing on language till now, from "The Way to Language." We feel all the more duty bound to do so since that text takes up the question of how human speaking, human language, is related to the language of stillness discussed above. In addition, let us try to understand a word which occupies the central point in the text, the word "event" (*Ereignis*).

The context in which this word occurs may be briefly indicated. "Language speaks in that it, as showing, reaching into all regions of presence, summons from them whatever is present to appear and to fade" (p. 124). The interconnection of language and letting-appear runs through all the texts dealing with language, from *Being and Time* to the last, although there is a change in the concept of letting-appear and of what it is that speaks. The speaker, man, can speak, according to Heidegger, only because he listens to language, and he can listen to it only because he belongs in it. "Saying grants the hearing, and thus the speaking, of language solely to those who belong within it" (p. 124). In this way Heidegger is able to single out granting as the basic feature of language. The relation of the speaker to language reminds us of the relation of Dasein to Being noted earlier. There, Heidegger stated that Dasein can only be by

the grace of Being but that, on the other hand, Being has need of
Dasein (compare the "Letter on 'Humanism'"). In the present
text we read: "Language needs human speaking, and yet it is not
merely of the making or at the command of our speech activity"
(p. 125).

The fundamental, underlying language, which Heidegger calls
"saying," enables all appearing. "Saying pervades and structures the
openness of that clearing which every appearance must seek out and
every disappearance must leave behind, and in which every present
or absent being must show, say, announce itself" (p. 126). Through
a consideration of what takes place in saying as thus conceived,
Heidegger comes upon the *Ereignis*, the event of appropriation or,
as this expression may also be rendered, the disclosure of appropriation.* It comes to pass, that is, there occurs, "the opening of the
clearing in which present beings can persist and from which absent
beings can depart while keeping their persistence in the withdrawal"
(p. 127). This granting should not be conceived on the model of
cause and effect. "There is nothing else from which the Appropriation itself could be derived, even less in whose terms it could be explained" (p. 127). This is what the eye, seeking to penetrate the
riddle of the giving of saying, of what saying gives, ultimately rests
upon. Elsewhere, Heidegger has said about Being that "it gives,"
but here he points out that it is the *Ereignis* that vouchsafes even
this "it gives," "of which even Being itself stands in need to come
into its own as presence" (p. 127).

The multiple possibilities of showing refer to saying as showing, and this in turn refers to the *Ereignis*, the mode of disclosure
in which appropriation occurs. It may be advisable to remember
here that the *Ereignis* cannot be hypostatized as an otherworldly
power standing above Being; we should rather try to grasp the
Ereignis as that which holds sway in language, .which we have encountered in our questing back into the showing of language. In

* In the meaning Heidegger reads into this word, there is a fusion of the
dictionary sense of a "happening," of "owning and appropriating" in *ereig-
nen* as suggested by the adjective *eigen* and the verb *aneignen*, and of er-
äugen (eying, seeing). For a full explanation, see Albert Hofstadter's remarks in the introduction to *Poetry, Language, Thought*, pp. xviii–xxi
(Tr.).

trying to reflect on the *Ereignis,* we by no means leave language behind. It is a new view of language which has been formed in light of the question as to how language lets man himself speak by opening up to him the clearing in which every entity is able to appear. This relationship should not in turn be conceived as if man were under the control of a power to which he must bow down; Heidegger only wants to exhibit what man owes to language as saying. For Heidegger, speaking proper is corresponding (*Ent-sprechen,* answering to)—corresponding to the saying and to the *Ereignis.* The relationship between Dasein and man mentioned before shows up again when Heidegger says that "man is used for bringing soundless Saying to the sound of language" (p. 129). (Compare what has been stated above on language as gathering.)

In speaking proper, what happens is nothing but a manifestation of the *Ereignis* which itself, however, remains hidden from the speaker himself. That is why experiencing in thought the nature of language is for Heidegger a laying open of the movement which leads from *Ereignis* to man's speech. Language has the power to bestow the clearing because it is in its very nature a granting appropriation (*Er-eignis,* making one's own). The moment of historicity, which is never abandoned in Heidegger's thinking, is present here also. The appropriation is not something that happens only once, not just a single event; it is capable of disclosing itself, of showing itself or withdrawing itself. It is in conformity with this showing-itself or denial that language happens and human speech itself changes.

"All human language is appropriated in Saying and as such is in the strict sense of the word true language—though its nearness to Appropriation may vary by various standards. All true language, because assigned, sent, destined to man by the way-making movement of Saying, is in the nature of destiny" (p. 133).

On the relationship between poetry and thought, Heidegger says, "All reflective thinking is poetic [*ein Dichten*], and all poetry in turn is a kind of thinking" (p. 136). We might add that, according to Heidegger, it is the *Ereignis* that is the real source of poetry (which poetizes in the true sense) and of which even language remains under the ownership, for which reason it could be spoken of as poetry in an earlier text.

41. Two-page spread of Heidegger's manuscript on "The Word"

42. Stefan George

43. Friedrich Wilhelm Joseph von Schelling, about 1850

44. Heidegger with the artist Bernhard Heiliger, October 1964

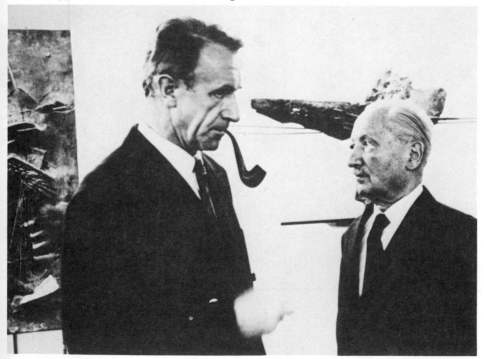

45. Friedrich Nietzsche

46. Georg Trakl

47. Sören Kierkegaard
(sketch by N. C. Kierkegaard)

50. A page from the manuscript of "Prüfung aus der Be-stimmung," written in the early 1960s

48 (left) and 49 (below). Heidegger and Rudolf Bultmann at the meeting of the "old Marburgers," 1961

51. Heidegger at Todtnauberg

52. Heidegger and his wife, 1961

53. The Heideggers at the cottage, October 1969

10

Aletheia—The Matter of Thinking ("The End of Philosophy and the Task of Thinking," 1964)

The text of this lecture was written in 1964. It appeared first in the collection *Kierkegaard Vivant* (Paris, 1966) in a translation by Jean Beaufret and François Fédier and was subsequently included in the volume *Zur Sache des Denkens* (1969; the English translation of this is *On Time and Being*). If we discuss it here at the end, it is because in it Heidegger looks backward as well as at the prospect ahead. The retrospective glance concerns philosophy as metaphysics, and the prospective look concerns the kind of thinking which no longer regards itself as metaphysics.

"Metaphysics thinks beings as beings in the manner of representational thinking which gives reasons" (p. 56).* Metaphysics seeks after the ground of beings, of what is; this ground it calls Being. Being is understood in the sense that it lets entities become present. This grounding can be conceived as causing or producing the real or actual (for example, God as the highest and ultimate ground), as the transcendental ground (for example, Kant's condition of the possibility of experience, which is at the same time the condition of the possibility of the objects of experience), as the dialectical movement of Absolute Spirit (in Hegel's sense), as

* Page references in this chapter are to *On Time and Being*, translated by Joan Stambaugh (New York: Harper & Row, 1972), which has in some cases been modified.

an explanation of the process of production (Marx), as Will to Power, which, in positing values, also posits itself (Nietzsche).

"What characterizes metaphysical thinking, which grounds the ground for beings, is the fact that metaphysical thinking, starting out from what is present, represents it in its presence and so describes it in terms of its ground as something grounded" (p. 56).

What, now, does the end of philosophy mean? It is not regarded as cessation in the sense of extinction but rather as the "place in which the whole of philosophy's history is gathered in its most extreme possibility" (p. 57). That is at the same time its completion. Completion here does not mean perfection but coming to an end. We cannot regard Kant's philosophy as more perfect than Plato's and the latter as more perfect than that of Parmenides. On the contrary, in every philosophy something finds expression which, in itself, possesses a necessity of its own. When we judge philosophy from the perspective of science, we easily fall prey to the illusion of regarding the earlier as always the imperfect, which we could even do without. This is not the proper way of looking at the history of philosophy. Plato's thought, for example, is not rendered superfluous by subsequent philosophies. The whole of metaphysics, on the contrary, is dominated throughout by Platonism, though a constantly changing Platonism, of which the final form is the reversal of Platonism in Nietzsche.

The development of philosophy is accompanied by the formation of the sciences, which then break away from philosophy. We are today in the midst of a process in which questions which were formerly dealt with by philosophy are increasingly passing into the realm of science. This might be viewed as a supplantation of philosophy by the sciences, but, according to Heidegger, it is rather a mark of the completion of metaphysics. For, modern metaphysics is actually the soil from which the sciences have emerged. The technological character of metaphysics in its phase of consummation (compare Chapter 8) has taken possession of the sciences. "The development of philosophy into the independent sciences which, however, interdependently communicate among themselves ever more markedly, is the legitimate completion of philosophy. Philosophy is ending in the present age. It has found its place in the scientific attitude of socially active humanity. But the fundamental characteristic of this scientific attitude is its cybernetic, that is, technological character" (p. 58). Heidegger elucidates this state of affairs, contradicting the common view, as follows: "The end of philosophy proves to be the triumph of the manipulable arrangement of a scientific-technological world and of the social order proper to this world. The end of philosophy means: the beginning of world civilization based upon Western European thinking" (p. 59).

The question that now arises is this. With the end of philosophy in the sense of its absorption into and going over to the sciences, are all its possibilities exhausted or is there still a possibility left which philosophy itself has not developed, a first possibility which lies hidden at the root of philosophy itself?

In order to be able to answer this question, we must not simply put philosophy aside but rather consider it in its historical unfolding, as Heidegger has done all his lifetime. Measured in terms of the philosophy of which the influence has entered into science and technology, what is attempted here is something very slight, a preparation for "a possibility whose contour remains obscure, whose coming remains uncertain" (p. 60). At the same time, it today strikes us as outrageous when Heidegger suggests "that the world civilization which is just now beginning might one day overcome the technological-scientific-industrial character as the sole criterion of man's world sojourn" (p. 60).

What is the "matter" of thinking, its concern? Heidegger goes into the views of two philosophers who have explicitly dealt with this question, Hegel and Husserl. It becomes evident that for both of them what is in dispute is not the matter—subjectivity—but the method. What remains unthought in this? Let us take Hegel's example. Speculative dialectic reveals how "the matter of philosophy comes to appear of itself and for itself, and thus becomes presence" (p. 64). Appearing presupposes some brightness in which what shines shows itself. Brightness in turn presupposes an openness, which it might illumine—openness as "free region." Openness is presupposed in speculative thought also, or, as Heidegger puts it, "Only this openness grants to the movement of speculative thinking the passage through that which it thinks" (pp. 64–65).

Heidegger conceives this openness as the clearing, the Lichtung (compare Chapters 5, 6 and 7). This word is formed on the analogy of the French clairère. Clearing, to open or lighten, means to make something free and open, like making a forest free of trees at some place. Light in the sense of brightness does not create the open but presupposes it in order that it may illumine something in this open sphere or "let brightness play with the darkness in it" (p. 65). "The clearing is the open for everything that is present and absent" (p. 65). The question should some day be asked "whether the opening, the free open, may not be that within which alone pure space and ecstatic time and everything present and absent in them have the place which gathers and protects everything" (p. 66).

Philosophizing is ever "already admitted to the free space of the opening . . . But philosophy knows nothing of the opening" (p. 66). This state of affairs was earlier called by Heidegger "the oblivion of Being." Presence—the basic word for Being as conceived by the Greeks—is always dependent on the clearing. And what is absent can also be experienced as absent only within the compass of the clearing. Plato conceived entities, it is true, in terms of their look or εἶδος and hence referred to light. "But there is no light and no brightness without the opening. Even darkness needs it" (p. 67).

In Parmenides' poem aletheia, unconcealedness, "is called well-rounded because it is turned in the pure sphere of the circle in which beginning and end are everywhere the same" (pp. 67–68).

Previously, Heidegger had shown that the path of thinking (of speculative philosophy as well as phenomenology) needs the clearing in order to come into being. He points out now that what is (a being) can become present, make its appearance, only thanks to this openness. What the clearing thus grants is twofold: the path on which the inquiry into what is may be conducted, in regard to its being present; and above all, the fact that what is itself achieves presence, that beings become present. "We must think aletheia, un-concealment, as the opening which first grants Being and thinking and their presencing to and for each other" (p. 68).

The question already posed in early Greek thought and one which remains a question for the entire metaphysical tradition—namely, how thinking and Being belong together—is here considered by Heidegger in terms of *aletheia*. We said at the beginning that the leitmotiv of Heidegger's thought is the question about Being and the question about truth. Here we see that *aletheia* exhibits itself as "the element in which Being and thinking and their belonging together exist" (p. 69). That of which there is a reminiscence in Parmenides is forgotten in metaphysics, which inquires into the Being of beings as their ultimate cause, in the sense of the highest being, and which is thus intrinsically onto-theological.

In the dimension of Heidegger's thinking the question has changed in such fashion that it is not the twofoldness of Being and truth that is now decisive but it is *aletheia* which emerges as the basis of Being as well as of truth. Truth as agreement of knowledge with what is—the traditional concept of truth—is only possible by virtue of standing in the clearing, as Heidegger first laid bare in "On the Essence of Truth." "For truth itself, just as Being and thinking, can only be what it is in the element of the opening. Evidence, certainty in every degree, every kind of verification of *veritas* already move *with* that *veritas* in the realm of the prevalent opening" (p. 69).

We have arrived at the point where *aletheia* shows itself as that primordial reality which we always overlook and leave out of consideration in favor of that which has arisen from it. *Aletheia* can no longer be equated with truth, for it is that which grants truth first of all—truth in the sense of correspondence or of the absolute certainty of knowledge. In this connection, Heidegger criticizes the attempt in *Being and Time*, from which we started out, in so far as it was based on translating *aletheia* as truth. And he also criticizes his own phrase "truth of Being" (as in "On the Essence of Truth" and the "Letter on 'Humanism' ").

Metaphysical thinking concerns itself with the various modes of presence of beings but not with what first of all leads to presence and is prior to it. There is presence only because of *aletheia*. Although the experience of *aletheia* was the element in which the Greeks lived, still even they did not expressly think it. Heidegger also corrects here his interpretation of Plato, according to which there took place, with Plato, a transformation of *aletheia* from its original sense of unconcealedness to correctness. He is now of the view that *aletheia* is directly, from the very first, interpreted in the light of correctness or rightness, and therefore does not come expressly into view. "Only what *aletheia* as opening grants is experienced and thought, not what it is as such" (p. 71). Man sticks to what is present and does not raise the question about presence and about the clearing which grants presence.

Why does this happen? Is it perhaps "because self-concealing, concealment, *Lethe* belongs to *Aletheia*" (p. 71)? "If this were so, then the opening would not be the mere opening of presence, but the opening of presence concealing itself, the opening of a self-concealing sheltering" (p. 71).

The questioning which inquires after this concealing is to be set in motion. Heidegger's whole endeavor is such setting-in-motion. It remains, of course, problematic whether we actually realize what goes on in such questioning, whether we are gripped by it, or remain, on the contrary, so fascinated by the technological-cybernetic form of representing that this kind of inquiry is bound to appear to us as pure fantasy.

Heidegger's work is a mountain range which we are not yet in a position to climb. We are able, it is true, to go some distance along this or that path and in the process catch sight of much that is unusual and exciting—but all that is a far cry from a direct hike to the ridge. The present work is intended to encourage attempts at coming closer to this mountain range. It had to limit itself to a few texts, and even these could not be explicated exhaustively. Should it have succeeded in bringing into view the unusual character of what this thinking is about, it has not been in vain. If it has at all been able to lead the reader to open his eyes to the unusual in what is accustomed, and if it succeeds in keeping away from Heidegger those who cling to what is accustomed, even that might be a justification for this inadequate and awkward exposition.

In regard to our present-day understanding of Heidegger, we may cite the words of a poet with whom a kind of "elective affinity" binds Heidegger—the lines from Hölderlin's "The Titans":

> But it is not
> The time. Yet . . .

Notes

1. Hannah Arendt, "Martin Heidegger zum 80. Geburtstag," *Merkur* 10 (1969): 893–902. English translation (E.T.), "Martin Heidegger at Eighty," *The New York Review of Books*, 21 October 1971.
2. See also the inaugural lecture to the Heidelberg Academy of Sciences included in the *Vorwort* to Martin Heidegger, *Frühe Schriften* (Frankfurt: Vittorio Klostermann, 1972). E. T., *Man and World* 3 (February 1970): 3–4.
3. See Otto Pöggeler, *Der Denkweg Martin Heideggers* (Pfullingen: Neske, 1963), Chapter 2, "Metaphysik und Geschichte."
4. See Hans Georg Gadamer, "Martin Heidegger und die Marburger Theologie," in *Heidegger*, ed. Otto Pöggeler (Köln and Berlin: Kiepenheur und Witsch, 1969), pp. 174–75.
5. Ibid., p. 169.
6. Ibid., p. 171: "The superb power of phenomenological intuition which Heidegger brought to bear upon his interpretation, liberated the original Aristotelian text so thoroughly and effectively from the deposits of the scholastic tradition and from the lamentably distorted image of Aristotle which the critical philosophy of the time had . . . that he began to speak to us in a quite unexpected manner." "Penetration to the original intention of the author" might perhaps be substituted for "power of phenomenological intuition."
7. Pöggeler, *Der Denkweg Martin Heideggers*, p. 7.
8. Heidegger presented this interpretation in a four-hours-a-week lecture course at Marburg in the winter semester of 1925–26, at the Herder Institute in Riga in September 1928 and at the Davos Institute for university teachers in March 1929. Heidegger's appearance at these courses attracted special notice.

9. On this problem, see Walter Biemel, *Le Concept de monde chez Heidegger* (Louvain: Nauwelaertes; Paris: Vrin, 1950).

10. See Walter Biemel, *Philosophische Analysen zur Kunst der Gegenwart*, Phaenomenologica, vol. 28 (The Hague: Nijhoff, 1969).

11. A careful exposition is to be found in J. L. Mehta, *The Philosophy of Martin Heidegger* (Varanasi: Banaras Hindu University Press, 1967), parts of which are included in an abridged edition of the book (New York: Harper & Row, 1971). Reference must also be made to the very thorough account in W. J. Richardson, *Heidegger. From Phenomenology to Thought*, Phaenomenologica, vol. 13 (The Hague: Nijhoff, 1963). Otto Pöggeler's *Der Denkweg Martin Heideggers* has been mentioned already. The "ontological difference" constitutes the central theme of the penetrating work by Alberto Rosales, *Transzendenz und Differenz*, Phaenomenologica, vol. 33 (The Hague: Nijhoff, 1970).

12. Pöggeler, *Der Denkweg Martin Heideggers*, p. 210.

13. Martin Heidegger delivered this lecture in October 1930 in Bremen, on 5 December of the same year in Marburg and on 11 December in Freiburg. It was repeated in Dresden in 1932. The text, first published in 1943, appears without alteration in *Wegmarken* (Frankfurt: Vittorio Klostermann, 1967), from which we quote.

14. The first version of the text was delivered as a lecture in November 1935 in Freiburg and in January 1936 in Zürich. The enlarged version was prepared in 1936 for three lectures, delivered in November and December of that same year, at the *Freie Deutsche Hochstift*.

15. As for the possible objection that art was already conceived of in terms of truth by Schelling and Hegel, see Walter Biemel, *Kants Begründung der Aesthetik und ihre Bedeutung für die Philosophie der Kunst* (*Kantstudien*, Supplementary Volume 66, 1960).

16. An attempt in this direction was made in Biemel, *Philosophische Analysen zur Kunst der Gegenwart*.

17. See Werner Heisenberg, *Die Künste im technischen Zeitalter* (München: Oldenbourg, 1954), pp. 43–69.

18. The notion of the fourfold cannot, unfortunately, be explained in greater detail here. The reader is referred to the article by Dieter Sinn, "Heideggers Spätphilosophie," *Philosophische Rundschau* 14, nos. 2–3 (1967), pp. 81–182; and to the article by Otto Pöggeler, "Sein als Ereignis," *Zeitschrift für philosophische Forschung* 13 (1959), pp. 597–632.

Chronology

1889   Martin Heidegger born 26 September, son of Friedrich Heidegger (1851–1924), head sexton and cellarman at Messkirch, and Johanna Heidegger, née Kempf (1858–1927).

1903–06   Attends the *Gymnasium* at Constance.

1906–09   Attends the *Gymnasium* at Freiburg.

1909–11   Studies theology in Freiburg.

1911–13   Studies philosophy, the humanities and science in Freiburg.

1913   Graduation under Schneider—Rickert as coexaminer—with a dissertation on *Die Lehre vom Urteil im Psychologismus*.

1916   Habilitation in Freiburg with the work *Die Kategorien und Bedeutungslehre des Duns Scotus*.

1917   Marries Elfriede Petri.

1919   Son Jörg born.

1920   Son Hermann born.

1922   Associate Professor at Marburg; remains at Marburg till 1928. Cottage in Todtnauberg built.

1923   "Dasein und Wachsein," lecture at the Kant Society in Cologne at the invitation of Max Scheler, repeated in Essen.

1926   "Begriff und Entwicklung der phänomenologischen Forschung," lecture at the Marburg Philosophy Circle, 4 December.

1927   *Sein und Zeit* (*Being and Time*) published.*

1928   Succeeds Edmund Husserl as Professor of Philosophy at the Albert-Ludwig University in Freiburg.

*Subsequent publications are not given here. They are included in the list of Heidegger's works, which begins on p. 187.

Kant und das Problem der Metaphysik, lecture series at the Herder Institute in Riga.

1929   "Philosophische Anthropologie und Metaphysik des Daseins," lecture in Frankfurt, 24 January.

Kant und das Problem der Metaphysik, lecture series at the Davos Institute for university teachers in March.

Address on the occasion of Edmund Husserl's seventieth birthday, 9 April.

"Was ist Metaphysik?," inaugural lecture, 24 July in the University Auditorium.

"Die heutige Problemlage der Philosophie," lecture in Karlsruhe in December.

1930   "Die Problemlage der heutigen Philosophie" and "Hegel und das Problem der Metaphysik," two lectures delivered at the Amsterdam Association of Higher Learning, 21 and 22 March.

"Vom Wesen der Wahrheit," lecture given in Bremen in October; in Marburg, 5 December; in Freiburg, 11 December; and in Dresden in 1932.

1933   Elected Rector of Albert-Ludwig University.

"Die Selbstbehauptung der deutschen Universität," speech given on the occasion of taking up the Rectorship on 27 May.

1934   Resigned rectorship.

1935   "Der Ursprung des Kunstwerkes," lecture given 13 November at the Society of Fine Arts, Freiburg; repeated in January 1936 in Zürich.

1936   "Hölderlin und das Wesen der Dichtung," lecture held in Rome, 2 April (published in *Erläuterungen zu Hölderlins Dichtung*).

Der Ursprung des Kunstwerkes, a series of three lectures held 17 and 24 November and 4 December in the Freie Deutsche Hochstift, Frankfurt (published in *Holzwege*).

1938   "Die Begründung des neuzeitlichen Weltbildes durch die Metaphysik," lecture at the Society for Fine Arts, Natural Science and Medicine in Freiburg, 9 June, as part of a series of lectures on The Establishment of the Modern World-Picture (see *Holzwege*, "Die Zeit des Weltbildes").

1939   "Hölderlins Hymne 'Wie wenn am Feiertage,'" lecture repeated several times during 1939 and 1940 (published in *Erläuterungen zu Hölderlins Dichtung*).

1940   "Platons Lehre von der Wahrheit," lecture (first published in *Jahrbuch für die geistige Überlieferung* in 1942; included in *Wegmarken*).

1943   "Andenken," written on the occasion of the centenary of Hölderlin's death for the Memorial Volume edited by P. Kluckhohn. "Heimkunft/An die Verwandten," address at the commemoration of Hölderlin's death centenary, 6 June at the University of Freiburg. (This and "Andenken" appear in *Erläuterungen zu Hölderlins Dichtung.*)
"Nietzsches Wort 'Gott ist tot,' " lecture given in a small circle (published in *Holzwege*).

1944   Drafted for compulsory national service (*Volkssturm*) in Autumn.

1945   Forbidden to teach until 1951 by the occupation forces.

1946   "Wozu Dichter?," lecture presented to a very small circle which met to commemorate the twentieth anniversary of Rilke's death (published in *Holzwege*).

1949   Einblick in Das, Was Ist, four lectures ("Das Ding," "Das Gestell," "Die Gefahr" and "Die Kehre") presented at the Bremen Club in December; repeated at Bühlerhöhe in 1950.

1950   "Das Ding," lecture (enlarged version) at the Bavarian Academy of Fine Arts, 6 June.
"Die Sprache," lecture at Bühlerhöhe, 7 October, in memory of Max Kommerell; repeated 14 February 1951 (published in *Unterwegs zur Sprache*).

1951   "Bauen Wohnen Denken," given as a lecture at the Darmstadt Symposium on Man and Space 5 August.
". . . dichterisch wohnet der Mensch . . . ," lecture at Bühlerhöhe 6 October.

1953   "Wer ist Nietzsches Zarathustra?" lecture, 8 May, at the Bremen Club.
"Wissenschaft und Besinnung," lecture, 15 May, on the occasion of the meeting of a study group of booksellers on scholarly subjects in Schauinsland, and 4 August, in Munich, preparatory to the Conference of the Bavarian Academy of Fine Arts on The Arts in the Technological Age.
"Die Frage nach der Technik," lecture, 18 November, at the Bavarian Academy of Fine Arts series The Arts in a Technological Age.

1954   "Die Frage nach der Technik" repeated 12 February in Freiburg on the 150th anniversary of Kant's death.
"Besinnung," lecture given in Zürich, Constance and, on 19 June, in Freiburg.

1955   "Gelassenheit," speech at the celebration of the composer Conradin Kreutzer's 175th birthday in Messkirch, 30 October.

"Was ist das—die Philosophie?," lecture in Cérisy-la-Salle in September.

1956   "Der Satz vom Grund," lecture, 25 May, at the Bremen Club, and 24 October, at the University of Vienna (published in *Der Satz vom Grund*).

"Gespräch mit Hebel beim *Schatzkästlein*," to celebrate Hebel Day.

"Paul Klee," lecture at a gathering of architects in Freiburg.

1957   "Die onto-theologische Verfassung der Metaphysik," lecture at Todtnauberg, 24 February (published in *Identität und Differenz*).

Grundsätze des Denkens, five lectures in the *Studium Generale* of the University of Freiburg in the Summer semester. The third lecture in this series, "Der Satz der Identität" was delivered as an address at the five-hundredth year Jubilee Celebrations of the Albert-Ludwig University on 27 June (published in *Identität und Differenz*).

Das Wesen der Sprache, three lectures in the *Studium Generale* of the University of Freiburg, 14 and 18 December and 7 February 1958 (published in *Unterwegs zur Sprache*).

1958   "Hegel et les Grecs," lecture in the *Nouvelle Faculté* of Aix-en-Provence, 20 March, and in German at the plenary meeting of the Heidelberg Academy of Sciences, 26 July (published in *Wegmarken*).

"Dichten und Denken. Zu Stefan Georges Gedicht 'Das Wort,'" lecture at a special morning function in the Burgtheater of Vienna, 11 May (*Unterwegs zur Sprache*).

1959   "Der Weg zur Sprache," lecture at the Bavarian Academy of Fine Arts, Munich, in January (*Unterwegs zur Sprache*).

Inaugural speech at the Heidelberg Academy of Sciences (published in *Jahreshefte der Heidelberger Akademie der Wissenschaften*, 1957/58; see also *Frühe Schriften*, Vorwort).

"Hölderlins Erde und Himmel," lecture held 6 June in Cuvilliés-Theater in Munich on the occasion of the meeting of the Hölderlin Society (published in *Erläuterungen zu Hölderlins Dichtung*, 4th ed., 1971).

"Dank an die Messkircher Heimat," speech on the occasion of being nominated honorary citizen of Messkirch, 27 September.

"Die Bestimmung der Künste im Gegenwärtigen Weltalter," lecture in Baden-Baden.

1960   "Sprache und Heimat," lecture in Wesselburen, 2 July.
1962   First trip to Greece.
1964   "Über Abraham a Santa Clara," speech, 2 May, in Martin's Hall, Messkirch.
1967   "Die Herkunft der Kunst und die Bestimmung des Denkens," lecture delivered 4 April at the Academy of Sciences and Arts in Athens.
1968   "Hölderlin: Das Gedicht," lecture in Amriswil; French translation read by René Char (published in *Erläuterungen zu Hölderlins Dichtung*, 4th ed., 1971).
        Hegel: Differenz des Fichteschen und Schellingschen Systems, Seminar in Thor (Provence) from 30 August to 8 September.
1969   Kant: Über den einzig möglichen Beweisgrund vom Dasein Gottes, Seminar in Thor (Provence) 2 to 11 September.
1976   Martin Heidegger dies 26 May.

Bibliography

BIBLIOGRAPHIES

1957 Lübbe, H. "Bibliographie der Heidegger-Literatur 1917–1955." *Zeitschrift für philosophische Forschung* 11.
1965 Ijsseling, S. "Van en over Heidegger. Kroniek van de Heideggerliteratuur 1955–1965." *Tijdschrift voor Filosofie* 27.
1968 Sass, H. M. *Heidegger-Bibliographie.* Meisenheim am Glan. [2,201 titles.]
1975 Sass, H.-M., et al. *Materialien zu einer Heidegger-Bibliographie.* Meisenheim am Glan. This supplement to Sass's earlier book contains 1,000 titles published between 1968 and 1972.

WORKS BY HEIDEGGER IN GERMAN

1912 "Das Realitätsproblem in der modernen Philosophie." *Philosophisches Jahrbuch* 25.
"Neuere Forschungen über Logik." *Literarische Rundschau für das katholische Deutschland* 38.
1914 *Die Lehre vom Urteil im Psychologismus. Ein kritisch-positiver Beitrag zur Logik.* Leipzig. [Dissertation].
1916 *Die Kategorien- und Bedeutungslehre des Duns Scotus.* Tübingen. [Habilitation thesis].

"Der Zeitbegriff in der Geschichtswissenschaft." *Zeitschrift für Philosophie und philosophische Kritik* 161.

1927 *Sein und Zeit. Erste Hälfte.* Jahrbuch für Philosophie und phänomenologische Forschung, vol. 8. Halle.

1929 *Was ist Metaphysik?* Bonn.

Kant und das Problem der Metaphysik. Bonn.

"Vom Wesen des Grundes." *Festschrift, Edmund Husserl zum 70. Geburtstag gewidmet.* Jahrbuch für Philosophie und phänomenologische Forschung. Halle.

1933 "Die Selbstbehauptung der deutschen Universität." Speech delivered upon Heidegger's assumption of the rectorship of Freiburg University, 27 May 1933. Breslau.

1936 "Hölderlin und das Wesen der Dichtung." *Das Innere Reich 3.*

1941 "Hölderlins Hymne 'Wie wenn am Feiertage . . .'" Halle.

1942 "Platons Lehre von der Wahrheit." *Geistige Überlieferung 2.*

1943 *Vom Wesen der Wahrheit.* Frankfurt.

"Andenken." *Hölderlin. Gedenkschrift zu seinem 100. Todestag.* Kluckhohn, P., ed. Tübingen.

1944 *Erläuterungen zu Hölderlins Dichtung.* Frankfurt. Contains: "Heimkunft/An die Verwandten." "Hölderlin und das Wesen der Dichtung" [reprint of 1936].

1947 *Platons Lehre von der Wahrheit. Mit einem Brief über den Humanismus.* Überlieferung und Auftrag. Reihe: Probleme und Hinweise, vol. 5. Bern. Contains: "Platons Lehre von der Wahrheit" [reprint of 1942], "Über den *Humanismus*" [letter to Jean Beaufret, in Paris].

1949 "Der Zuspruch des Feldweges." *Sonntagsblatt,* 23 Oktober.

1950 *Holzwege.* Frankfurt. 1950.

Contains: "Der Ursprung des Kunstwerkes," "Die Zeit des Weltbildes," "Hegels Begriff der Erfahrung," "Nietzsches Wort 'Gott ist tot,'" "Wozu Dichter," and "Der Spruch des Anaximander."

1951 Letter to Emil Staiger, in Staiger, Emil. "Zu einem Vers von Mörike. Ein Briefwechsel mit Martin Heidegger." *Trivium 9.*

"Logos." In *Festschrift für Hans Jantzen.* Berlin, pp. 7–18.

"Das Ding." *Gestalt und Gedanke. Ein Jahrbuch.* Bayerischen Akademie der Schönen Künste. München.

1952 "Bauen Wohnen Denken." In *Mensch und Raum.* Darmstädter Gespräch, vol. 2. Darmstadt.

"Was heißt Denken?" *Merkur 6.*

1953 Einführung in die Metaphysik. Tübingen.
"Georg Trakl. Eine Eröterung seines Gedichtes." Merkur 7.
1954 Aus der Erfahrung des Denkens. Pfullingen.
". . . dichterisch wohnet der Mensch . . ." Akzente 1.
"Heraklit." Festschrift zur Feier des 350jährigen Bestehens des Heinrich-Suso-Gymnasiums in Konstanz. Konstanz.
"Die Frage nach der Technik." In Gestalt und Gedanke, vol. 3.
Bayerischen Akademie der Schönen Künste. München.
"Wissenschaft und Besinnung." Börsenblatt für den Deutschen Buchhandel. 13 April 1954.
"Anmerkungen über die Metaphysik." Im Umkreis der Kunst. Eine Festschrift für Emil Preetorius. Wiesbaden.
Vorträge und Aufsätze. Pfullingen. Contains: I. "Die Frage nach der Technik." [reprint of 1954], "Wissenschaft und Besinnung." [reprint of 1954], "Überwindung der Metaphysik," "Wer ist Nietzsches Zarathustra?"; II. "Was heißt Denken?" [reprint of 1952], "Bauen Wohnen Denken" [reprint of 1952], "Das Ding" [reprint of 1951], with an epilogue entitled "Ein Brief an einen jungen Studenten," ". . . dichterisch wohnet der Mensch . . ." [reprint of 1954]; III. "Logos (Heraklit, Fragment 50)" [reprint of 1951], "Moira (Parmenides, Fragment VIII, 34–41)" [in part reprinted from "Was heißt Denken?," 1952], "Aletheia (Heraklit, Fragment 16)" [reprint of "Heraklit," 1954].
Was heißt Denken? Tübingen.
1955 "Über Die Linie." Freundschaftliche Begegnungen. Festschrift für Ernst Jünger zum 60. Geburtstag. Frankfurt.
1956 Was ist das—die Philosophie? Pfullingen.
Zur Seinsfrage [reprint of Über Die Linie, 1955]. Frankfurt.
"Der Satz vom Grund." Wissenschaft und Weltbild 9.
Gespräch mit Hebel. Mein Schatzkästlein zum Hebeltag 1956. From Schriftenreihe des Hebelbundes, vol. 4. Lörrach.
1957 Der Satz vom Grund. Pfullingen. [Includes reprint of 1956.]
"Der Satz der Identität." In Die Albert-Ludwigs-Universität Freiburg 1457–1957. Die Festvorträge bei der Jubiläumsfeier. Freiburg.
Identität und Differenz. Pfullingen.
Contains: "Der Satz der Identität" [reprint of 1957], "Die onto-theo-logische Verfassung der Metaphysik."
Hebel als Hausfreund. Pfullingen. [Enlarged version of "Gespräch mit Hebel," 1956.]

1958 "Grundsätze des Denkens." In *Jahrbuch für Psychologie und Psychotherapie*. Vol. 6.

"Vom Wesen und Begriff der PHYSIS, Aristoteles *Physik B 1*." In *Il Pensiero*. Vol. 3. Milano.

1959 *Gelassenheit*. Pfullingen. Contains: "Gelassenheit," "Zur Erörterung der Gelassenheit. Aus einem Feldweggespräch über das Denken."

"Der Weg zur Sprache." In *Gestalt und Gedanke*. Vol. 5. Bayerischen Akademie der Schönen Künste. München.

"Hegel et les Grecs." Translated by J. Beaufret and P.-P. Sagave. *Cahiers du Sud*, année 45, no. 349.

Unterwegs zur Sprache. Pfullingen. Contains: "Die Sprache," "Die Sprache im Gedicht. Eine Erörterung von Georg Trakls Gedicht" [reprint of "Georg Trakl," 1953], "Aus einem Gespräch von der Sprache. Zwischen einem Japaner und einem Fragenden," "Das Wesen der Sprache," "Das Wort," "Der Weg zur Sprache" [reprint of 1959].

1960 "Hölderlins Erde und Himmel." *Hölderlin-Jahrbuch* 11 (1958–1960).

"Sprache und Heimat." In: *Hebbel-Jahrbuch* 1960. Heide 1960. S. 27–50.

"Hegel und die Griechen." In *Die Gegenwart der Griechen im neueren Denken. Festschrift für Hans Georg Gadamer zum 60. Geburtstag*. Tübingen. [Translation of "Hegel et les Grecs," 1959.]

1961 *Nietzsche*. Erster Band. Pfullingen. Contains: "Der Wille zur Macht als Kunst," "Die ewige Wiederkehr des Gleichen" and "Der Wille zur Macht als Erkenntnis."

Nietzsche. Zweiter Band. Pfullingen. Contains: "Die ewige Wiederkehr des Gleichen und der Wille zur Macht," "Der europäische Nihilismus," "Nietzsches Metaphysik," "Die seinsgeschichtliche Bestimmung des Nihilismus," "Die Metaphysik als Geschichte des Seins," "Entwürfe zur Geschichte des Seins als Metaphysik" and "Die Erinnerung an die Metaphysik."

"Dank an die Meßkircher Heimat." Speech given by Professor Martin Heidegger on the occasion of being named honorary citizen of the town of Messkirch on 27 September 1959. In *Meßkirch gestern und heute. Heimatbuch zum 700-jährigen Stadtjubiläum*. Messkirch.

"Sprache und Heimat." In *Dauer im Wandel. Festschrift zum 70. Geburtstag von Carl Jacob Burckhardt.* München. (Abridged version of 1960 essay.)

1962 *Die Frage nach dem Ding. Zu Kants Lehre von den transzendentalen Grundsätzen.* Tübingen.

"Kants These über das Sein." In *Existenz und Ordnung. Festschrift für Erik Wolf zum 60. Geburtstag.* Frankfurt.

Die Technik und die Kehre. Opuscula aus Wissenschaft und Dichtung, 1. Pfullingen. Contains: "Die Frage nach der Technik" [reprint of 1954] and "Die Kehre."

1963 "Ein Vorwort." Letter to William J. Richardson. In W. J. Richardson. *Heidegger. Through Phenomenology to Thought.* Phaenomenologica. Vol. 13. The Hague.

1964 "Aus der letzten Marburger Vorlesung." [On Leibniz.] In *Zeit und Geschichte. Dankesgabe an Rudolf Bultmann zum 80. Geburtstag.* Tübingen.

Über Abraham a Santa Clara. Stadt Meßkirch. Meßkirch.

1967 *Wegmarken.* Frankfurt. Contains reprints of twelve essays written between 1929 and 1964.

Der europäische Nihilismus. Pfullingen. Contains reprints of two essays written in 1961.

1968 "Zeit und Sein." In *L'endurance de la pensée—Pour saluer Jean Beaufret.* Paris.

1969 *Die Kunst und der Raum.—L'art et l'espace.* Translated by Jean Beaufret and François Fédier. Sankt Gallen.

Zur Sache des Denkens. Tübingen. Contains: "Zeit und Sein" [reprint of 1968], "Protokoll zu einem Seminar über den Vortrag "Zeit und Sein," "Das Ende der Philosophie und die Aufgabe des Denkens" [first published, in French, in *Kierkegaard vivant*, 1966] and "Mein Weg in die Phänomenologie" [first printed privately in 1963].

1970 *Heraklit.* Seminar, Winter semester, 1966–67. Eugen Fink, joint author. Frankfurt.

Phänomenologie und Theologie. Frankfurt.

1971 *Schellings Abhandlung Über das Wesen der menschlichen Freiheit* ⟨1809⟩. Edited by Hildegard Feick. Tübingen.

1972 *Frühe Schriften.* Frankfurt. Contains: "Die Lehre vom Urteil im Psychologismus," "Die Kategorien- und Bedeutungslehre des Duns Scotus" and "Der Zeitbegriff in der Geschichtswissenchaft" [all reprints].

1975 Die Grundprobleme der Phänomenologie (Martin Heidegger: Gesamtausgabe, II Abteilung, Band 24). Lecture course, Summer semester, 1927. Edited by F. W. von Herrmann. Frankfurt.
1976 Logik. Die Frage nach der Wahrheit (Martin Heidegger: Gesamtausgabe, II Abteilung, Band 21). Lecture course, Winter semester, 1925/26. Edited by Walter Biemel. Frankfurt.

ENGLISH TRANSLATIONS OF HEIDEGGER'S WORK

1949 Existence and Being. Introduction by Werner Brock. Contains: "Remembrance of the Poet" and "Hölderlin and the Essence of Poetry," translated by Douglas Scott; "On the Essence of Truth" and "What is Metaphysics?," translated by R. F. C. Hull and Alan Crick. Chicago: Regnery.
1951 "The Age of the World View." Translated by Marjorie Grene. Measure 2 (1951).
1957 "The Way Back into the Ground of Metaphysics." Translated by Walter Kaufmann. In Kaufmann, Walter, ed. Existentialism. New York: Meridian.
1958 What is Philosophy? Translated by William Kluback and Jean T. Wilde. With German text. New York: Twayne.
    The Question of Being. Translated by William Kluback and Jean T. Wilde. With German text. New York: Twayne.
1959 Introduction to Metaphysics. Translated by Ralph Manheim. New Haven: Yale University Press.
1962 Being and Time. Translated by John Macquarrie and Edward Robinson. New York: Harper & Row.
    Kant and the Problem of Metaphysics. Translated by James S. Churchill. Bloomington, Ind.: Indiana University Press.
    "Plato's Doctrine of Truth," translated by John Barlow, and "Letter on 'Humanism,'" translated by Edgar Lohner. In Barrett, William, and Aiken, Henry D., eds. Philosophy in the Twentieth Century. New York: Random House.
1966 Discourse on Thinking. Translated by John M. Anderson and E. Hans Freund. New York: Harper & Row.
1967 What is a Thing? Translated by W. B. Barton, Jr. and Vera Deutsch. Chicago: Regnery.

1968 *What is Called Thinking?* Translated by Fred E. Wieck and J. Glenn Gray. New York: Harper & Row.

1969 *The Essence of Reasons.* Translated by Terrence Malick. With German text. Evanston, Ill.: Northwestern University Press.

Identity and Difference. Translated by Joan Stambaugh. With German text. New York: Harper & Row.

1970 *Hegel's Concept of Experience.* New York: Harper & Row.

Inaugural address at the Heidelberg Academy of Science. In Siegfried, Hans, "Martin Heidegger: A Recollection," *Man and World 3.*

1971 *On the Way to Language.* Contains: "A Dialogue on Language," "The Nature of Language," "The Way to Language" and "Language in the Poem," translated by Joan Stambaugh; "Words," translated by Peter D. Hertz. New York: Harper & Row.

Poetry, Language, Thought. Translated by Albert Hofstadter. Contains: "The Thinker as Poet," "The Origin of the Work of Art," "What are Poets for?," "Building Dwelling Thinking," "The Thing," "Language" and ". . . Poetically Man Dwells. . . ." New York: Harper & Row.

1972 *On Time and Being.* Translated by Joan Stambaugh. Contains: "Time and Being," "Summary of a Seminar on the Lecture 'Time and Being,'" "The End of Philosophy and the Task of Thinking" and "My Way to Phenomenology." New York: Harper & Row.

1973 *The End of Philosophy.* Translated by Joan Stambaugh. Contains: "Metaphysics as History of Being," "Sketches for a History of Being as Metaphysics," "Recollections in Metaphysics" and "Overcoming Metaphysics." New York: Harper & Row.

"Art and Space." Translated by Charles H. Seibert. *Man and World 6.*

"The Problem of Reality in Modern Philosophy." Tranlated by Philip J. Bossert. *Journal of the British Society for Phenomenology 4.*

"The Pathway." Translated by Thomas F. O'Meara, O.P. Revised by Thomas J. Sheehan. *Listening—Journal of Religion and Culture 8,* Nos. 1, 2, 3, which also includes 'Messkirch's Seventh Centennial." Translated by Thomas J. Sheehan.

"Kant's Thesis about Being." Translated by Ted E. Klein, Jr. and William E. Pohl. *The Southwestern Journal of Philosophy 4* (Heidegger Issue).

1974 "The Anaximander Fragment." Translated by David Farrell Krell. *Arion* n.s. 1 (1973/1974).

1975 *Early Greek Thinking*. Translated by David Farrell Krell and Frank A. Capuzzi. Contains: "The Anaximander Fragment," "Logos (Heraclitus, Fragment B 50)," "Moira (Parmenides VIII, 34–41)" and "Aletheia (Heraclitus, Fragment B 16)." New York: Harper & Row.

1976 *Martin Heidegger: Basic Writings. From Being and Time* (1927) *to the Task of Thinking* (1964). Edited and introduced by David Farrell Krell. New York: Harper & Row.

The Question concerning Technology and Other Essays. Translated by William Lovitt. Contains: "The Question concerning Technology," "The Turning," "The Word of Nietzsche: 'God is Dead,' " "The Age of the World Picture," and "Science and Reflection." New York: Harper & Row.

GENERAL ACCOUNTS
OF HEIDEGGER'S PHILOSOPHY

1942 Waelhens, A. de. *La philosophie de Martin Heidegger*. Louvain. [Reprint, 1946. 5th ed., 1967.]

1947 Naber, A. "Von der Philosophie des *Nichts* zur Philosophie des *Seins-selbst*. Zur großen *Wende* im Philosophieren M. Heideggers." In *Gregorianum*, vol. 28. Rome.

1949 Bröcker, W. "Über die geschichtliche Notwendigkeit der Heideggerschen Philosophie." In *Actas del primer Congreso nacional de Filosofía*, vol 2. Mendoza.

1951 Diemer, A. "Grundzüge des Heideggerschen Philosophierens." In *Zeitschrift für philosophische Forschung* 5 (1950/51).

1959 Langan, Th. *The meaning of Heidegger. A critical study of an existentialist phenomenology*. New York.

1961 Vycinas, V. *Earth and Gods. An introduction to the philosophy of Martin Heidegger*. The Hague.

1963 Pöggeler, O. *Der Denkweg Martin Heideggers*. Pfullingen.

Richardson, W. J. *Heidegger. Through phenomenology to thought*. Preface by Martin Heidegger. Phaenomenologica, vol. 13. The Hague.

1964 Herrmann, F. W. von. *Die Selbstinterpretation Martin Heideggers.*
Monographien zur philosophischen Forschung, vol. 32. Meisenheim am Glan.

Ijsseling, S. *Heidegger. Denken en danken—geven en zijn.* Filosofie
en kultuur, vol. 2. Antwerpen.

King, M. *Heidegger's philosophy: A guide to his basic thought.* New
York.

1965 Kockelmans, J. J. *Martin Heidegger. A first introduction to his philosophy.* Pittsburgh and Louvain.

Waelhens, A. de. "Reflexions on Heidegger's development. A propos
of a recent book." *International Philosophical Quarterly* 5.

1967 Sinn, D. "Heideggers Spätphilosophie." *Philosophische Rundschau* 15.

1971 Mehta, J. L. *The Philosophy of Martin Heidegger.* New York and
Louvain.

1976 Mehta, J. L. *Martin Heidegger: The Way and The Vision.* Hono-
lulu: The University Press of Hawaii.

SOME EVALUATIONS

1946 Gandillac, M. de. "Entretien avec Martin Heidegger." *Les temps
modernes* 1, 4 (1945/46).

1949 Lukács, G. "Heidegger redivivus." *Sinn und Form* 1,3.

1953 Löwith, K. *Heidegger, Denker in dürftiger Zeit.* Frankfurt.

1966 Erickson, S. A. "Martin Heidegger." *Review of Metaphysics* 19
(1965/66).

COMMEMORATIVE VOLUMES AND ARTICLES

1949 *Martin Heideggers Einfluß auf die Wissenschaften. Aus Anlaß seines
60. Geburtstages.* Edited by Carlos Astrada, et al. Bern. Includes:
Astrada, C., "Über die Möglichkeit einer existenzialgeschicht-
lichen Praxis"; Bauch, K., "Die Kunstgeschichte und die heutige
Philosophie"; Binswanger, L., "Die Bedeutung der Daseinsanaly-
tik Martin Heideggers für das Selbstverständnis der Psychiatrie";
Heiss, R., "Psychologismus, Psychologie und Hermeneutik";
Kunz, H., "Die Bedeutung der Daseinsanalytik Martin Heideg-
gers für die Psychologie und die philosophische Anthropologie";
Ruprecht, E., "Heideggers Bedeutung für die Literaturwissen-

schaft"; Schadewaldt, W., "Odysseus-Abenteuer. Aus einer gesprächsweisen homerischen Improvisation über Irrfahrer-Angelegenheiten"; Schrey, H.-H., "Die Bedeutung der Philosophie Martin Heideggers für die Theologie"; Staiger, E., "Zu Klopstocks Ode 'Der Zürchersee' "; Szilasi, W., "Interpretation und Geschichte der Philosophie"; and Weizsäcker, C. F. von, "Beziehungen der theoretischen Physik zum Denken Heideggers."

1950 *Anteile. Martin Heidegger zum 60. Geburtstag.* Frankfurt. Includes: Bröcker, W., "Der Mythos vom Baum der Erkenntnis"; Gadamer, H. G., "Zur Vorgeschichte der Metaphysik"; Guardini, R., "Leib und Leiblichkeit in Dantes 'Göttlicher Komödie' "; Jünger, E., "Über die Linie"; Jünger, F. G., "Die Wildnis"; Krüger, G., "Über Kants Lehre von der Zeit"; Löwith, K., "Weltgeschichte und Heilsgeschehen"; Otto, W. F., "Die Zeit und das Sein"; Volkmann-Schluck, K. H., "Zur Gottesfrage bei Nietzsche"; and Wolf, E., "ANHP ΔΙΚΑΙΟΣ."

1959 *Martin Heidegger zum siebzigsten Geburtstag. Festschrift.* Edited by Günther Neske. Pfullingen. Includes:

PHILOSOPHY—Beaufret, J., "La fable du monde"; Bröcker, W., "Zu Hölderlins Ödipus-Deutung"; Gadamer, H. G., "Vom Zirkel des Verstehens"; Guzzoni, A., "Ontologische Differenz und Nichts"; Peursen, C. A. van, "Die Kommunikationshaftigkeit der Welt"; Schulz, W., "Hegel und das Problem der Aufhebung der Metaphysik"; Tanabe, H. "Todesdialektik"; Volkmann-Schluck, K. H., "Der Satz vom Widerspruch als Anfang der Philosophie"; Wagner de Reyna, A., "Die Enttäuschung"; and Weizsäcker, C. F. von, "Allgemeinheit und Gewissheit."

THEOLOGY—Bultmann, R., "Erziehung und christlicher Glaube"; Lotz, J. B., "Das Sein selbst und das subsistierende Sein nach Thomas von Aquin"; and Schlier, H., "Meditationen über den johannischen Begriff der Wahrheit."

LITERATURE AND FINE ARTS—Allemann, B., "Der Ort war aber die Wüste"; Blanchot, M., "L'Altenti"; Jens, W., "Marginalien zur modernen Literatur"; Petzel, H. W., " 'Reif ist die Traube und festlich die Luft' "; Preetorius, E., "Vom Geheimnis des Sichtbaren"; Schadewaldt, W., "Pindars zehnte nemeische Ode"; and Schmidt, G., "Naturalismus und Realismus."

MEDICINE AND PHYSICS—Boss, M., "Martin Heidegger und die Ärzte"; and Heisenberg, W., "Grundlegende Voraussetzungen in der Physik der Elementarteilchen."

POETRY AND APPLIED ARTS—Aichinger, I., "Versuch"; Arp, H., print; Braque, G., Dedication; Char, R., Dedication; Eich, G., "Altes Buch"; Grieshaber, H., "Martin Heidegger zum 70. Geburtstag"; Heissenbüttel, H., "Einsätze"; Jünger, E., "Vom Ende des geschichtlichen Zeitalters"; Jünger, F G., "Abendgang"; Podewils, C., "Der Steig"; and Podewils, S. D., "Chrysaora."

1969 *Heidegger*. Edited by Otto Pöggeler. Perspektiven zur Deutung seines Werks. Köln and Berlin. Introduction, "Heidegger heute"; Allemann, B., "Martin Heidegger und die Politik"; Anz, W., "Die Stellung der Sprache bei Heidegger"; Apel, K.-O., "Wittgenstein und Heidegger. Die Frage nach dem Sinn von Sein und der Sinnlosigkeitsverdacht gegen alle Metaphysik"; Becker, O., "Para-Existenz. Menschliches Dasein und Dawesen"; Bröcker, W., "Heidegger und die Logik"; Franz, H., "Das Denken Heideggers und die Theologie"; Gadamer, H. G., "Martin Heidegger und die Marburger Theologie"; Löwith, K., "Phänomenologische Ontologie und protestantische Theologie"; Lehmann, K., "Christliche Geschichtserfahrung und ontologische Frage beim jungen Heidegger"; Müller, M., "Phänomenologie, Ontologie und Scholastik"; Perpeet, W., "Heideggers Kunstlehre"; Pöggeler, O., "Hermeneutische und mantische Philosophie"; Schulz, W., "Über den philosophiegeschichtlichen Ort Martin Heideggers"; Staiger, E., "Ein Rückblick"; and Tugendhat, E., "Heideggers Idee von Wahrheit."

Martin Heidegger zum 80. Geburtstag von seiner Heimatstadt Meßkirch. Frankfurt.

Arendt, H. "Martin Heidegger zum 80. Geburtstag." *Merkur* 10.

1970 *Durchblicke. Martin Heidegger zum 80. Geburtstag.* Edited by Vittorio Klostermann. Frankfurt. Includes:
Boehm, R., "ΧΙΑΣΜΑ. Merleau-Ponty und Heidegger"; Fahrenbach, H., "Heidegger und das Problem einer 'philosophischen' Anthropologie"; Granel, G., "Remarques sur le rapport de Sein und Zeit et de la phénoménologie husserlienne"; Harries, K., "Das befreite Nichts"; Heftrich, E., "Nietzsche im Denken Heideggers"; Held, K., "Der Logos-Gedanke des Heraklit"; Herrmann, Fr.-W. von, "Sein und Cogitationes. Zu Heideggers Descartes-Kritik"; Hirsch, W., "Platon und das Problem der Wahrheit"; Hoppe, W., "Wandlungen in der Kant-Auffassung Heideggers"; Janke, W., "Die Zeitlichkeit der Repräsentation. Zur Seinsfrage bei Leibniz"; Jonas, H., "Wandlung und Bestand. Vom Grunde der Verstehbarkeit des Geschichtlichen";

Orr, H., "Die Bedeutung von Martin Heideggers Denken für die Methode der Theologie"; Patočka, J., "Heidegger vom anderen Ufer"; Petrović, G., "Der Spruch des Heidegger"; Schulz-Seitz, R.-E., "Bevestigter Gesang—Bemerkungen zu Heideggers Hölderlin-Auslegung"; Taminiaux, J., "Dialectique et différence"; and Tugendhat, E., " 'Das Sein und das Nichts.' "

APPRECIATION AND CRITICISM

1948 Waelhens, A. de. "La philosophie de Heidegger et le nazisme." Les temps modernes 3 (1947/48).
Löwith, K. "Réponse à M. De Waelhens." Les temps modernes 4.
Waelhens, A. de. "Réponse à cette réponse." Les temps modernes 4.
1961 Hühnerfeld, P. In Sachen Heidegger. München.
1962 Schneeberger, G. Nachlese zu Heidegger. Dokumente zu seinem Leben und Denken. Bern.
1964 Adorno, Th. W. Jargon der Eigentlichkeit. Zur deutschen Ideologie. Frankfurt.
1965 Schwan, A. Die politische Philosophie im Denken Heideggers. Ordo politicus, vol. 2. Köln and Opladen.
1966 Fédier, F. "Trois attaques contre Heidegger." Critiques 234.
1968 Palmier, J.-M. Les écrits politiques de Heidegger. L'Herne.
1970 Martin Heidegger im Gespräch. Edited by Richard Wisser. Radio broadcasts on the eightieth birthday of Martin Heidegger, 26 September 1969. Freiburg and München.
1972 Pöggeler, O. Philosophie und Politik bei Heidegger. Freiburg and München.

STUDIES ON HEIDEGGER

HEIDEGGER AND THE PHILOSOPHICAL TRADITION

1946 Alquie, F. "Existentialisme et philosophie chez Heidegger." La revue internationale 10.
Waelhens, A. de "Heidegger et J.-P. Sartre. Deucalion 1.

1948 Delfgaauw, B. "Heidegger en Sartre." *Tijdschrift voor Philosophie* 10.

Löwith, K. "Heidegger: Problem and background of existentialism." *Social Research* 15.

Merlan, Ph. "Time consciousness in Husserl and Heidegger." *Philosophy and Phenomenological Research* 8 (1947/48).

Peursen, C. A. van. *Riskante Philosophie. Een karakteristiek van het hedendaagse existentielle denken.* Amsterdam.

Waelhens, A. de "Heidegger, Platon et l'humanisme." *Revue philosophique de Louvain* 46.

1949 Dufrenne, M. "Heidegger et Kant." *Revue de métaphysique et de morale* 54.

Gurvitch, G. *Les tendences actuelles de la philosophie allemande. E. Husserl; M. Scheler; E. Lask; M. Heidegger.* Paris.

Levinas, E. *En découvrant l'existence avec Husserl et Heidegger.* Paris.

Müller, M. *Existenzphilosophie im geistigen Leben der Gegenwart.* Heidelberg.

Wahl, J., and Jankélévitch, V. "Les philosophes et l'angoisse." [On Heidegger, Jaspers.] *Revue de Synthèse Historique* 25.

1950 Biemel, W. "Husserls Enzyclopaedia-Britannica-Artikel und Heideggers Anmerkungen dazu." [With extracts from a letter from Heidegger to Husserl.] *Tijdschrift voor Philosophie* 12.

Jolivet, R. *Le problème de la mort chez Martin Heidegger et J.-P. Sartre.* Abbaye S. Wandrille.

1951 Gabriel, L. *Existenzphilosophie. Von Kierkegaard bis Sartre.* Wien.

1952 Knittermeyer, H. *Die Philosophie der Existenz von der Renaissance bis zur Gegenwart.* Wien and Stuttgart.

Pfeiffer, J. *Existenzphilosophie. Einführung in Heidegger und Jaspers.* 3rd ed. Hamburg.

1953 Hommes, J. *Zwiespältiges Dasein. Die existenziale Ontologie von Hegel bis Heidegger.* Freiburg.

Meulen, J. van der. *Heidegger und Hegel oder Widerstreit und Widerspruch.* Meisenheim am Glan.

Waelhens, A. de. *Phénoménologie et vérité. Essai sur l'évolution de l'idée de vérité chez Husserl et Heidegger.* Paris.

1954 Vuillemin, J. *L'héritage Kantien et la révolution copernicienne. Fichte, Cohen, Heidegger.* Paris.

1955 Marx, W. "Heidegger's new conception of philosophy. The second phase of Existentialism." *Social Research* 22.

1958 Hommes, J. *Krise der Freiheit. Hegel—Marx—Heidegger.* Regensburg.

Birault, H. "L'onto-theo-logique hegelienne et la dialetique." *Tijdschrift voor Philosophie* 20.

1959 Siewerth, G. *Das Schicksal der Metaphysik von Thomas zu Heidegger.* Horizonte, Vol. 6. Einsiedeln.

1960 Spiegelberg, H. *The phenomenological movement. A historical introduction.* Phaenomenologica, vol. 5. The Hague.

1961 Hübscher, A. *Von Hegel zu Heidegger. Gestalten und Probleme.* Stuttgart.

Marx, W. *Heidegger und die Tradition. Eine problemgeschichtliche Einführung in die Grundbestimmungen des Seins.* Stuttgart.

Theunissen, M. "Intentionaler Gegenstand und ontologische Differenz. Ansätze zur Fragestellung Heideggers in der Phänomenologie Husserls." *Philosophisches Jahrbuch* 70 (1962/63).

1963 Behl, L. "Wittgenstein und Heidegger." *Duns Scotus Philosophical Association* 27.

Rioux, B. "La notion de vérité chez Heidegger et Saint Thomas d'Aquin." In *S. Thomas d'Aquin aujourd'hui.* Coll. Recherches de Philosophie, vol. 6. Brugges.

1964 Schultz, U. *Das Problem des Schematismus bei Kant und Heidegger.* [Dissertation.] München.

Seidel, G. J. *Martin Heidegger and the Pre-Socratics. An introduction to his thought.* Lincoln, Neb.

1967 Gadamer, H. G. "Anmerkungen zu dem Thema Hegel und Heidegger." In *Natur und Geschichte. Karl Löwith zum 70. Geburtstag.* Stuttgart.

Tugendhat, E. *Der Wahrheitsbegriff bei Husserl und Heidegger.* Berlin.

Wisser, R. *Verantwortung im Wandel der Zeit. Jaspers, Buber, v. Weizsäcker, Guardini, Heidegger.* Mainz.

CENTRAL PROBLEMS OF HEIDEGGER'S PHILOSOPHY

BEING—TRUTH—ONTOLOGICAL DIFFERENCE

1947 Beaufret, J. "Heidegger et le problème de la vérité." *Fontaine* 63.

Welte, B. "Remarques sur l'ontologie de Heidegger. *Revue des sciences philosophiques et théologiques* 31.

1948 Fink, E. "Philosophie als Überwindung der Naivität. (Bruchstücke einer Vorlesung zum Begriff der ontologischen Differenz bei Heidegger.)" Lexis 1.

Gaos, J. "El ser y el tiempo de Martin Heidegger." Filosofía y Letras 16.

Lohmann, J. "M. Heideggers Ontologische Differenz und die Sprache." Lexis 1.

1949 Biemel, W. "Heideggers Begriff des Daseins." Studia Catholica 24.

Brock, W. Introduction, Martin Heidegger, Existence and Being. London.

Fink, E. "Zum Problem der ontologischen Erfahrung." Actas del primer Congreso nacional de Filosofía 2.

1950 Apel, K. O. Dasein und Erkennen. Eine erkenntnistheoretische Interpretation der Philosophie Martin Heideggers. [Dissertation.] Bonn.

Biemel, W. Le concept de monde chez Heidegger. Louvain and Paris.

Ceñal, R. "El problema de la verdad en Heidegger." Sapientia 5.

Vietta, E. Die Seinsfrage bei Martin Heidegger. Stuttgart.

1951 Birault, H. "Existence et vérité d'après Heidegger." Revue de métaphysique et de morale 56. Reprinted in Phénoménologie et Existence. Recueil d'études by H. Birault, et al. Paris.

Ohms, J. F. Der Begriff der ontologischen Wahrheit bei Martin Heidegger. Seine Voraussetzungen und Konsequenzen. [Dissertation.] Graz.

Peursen, C. A. van. "De Philosophie van Martin Heidegger als Wending tot het Zijn." Tijdschrift voor Philosophie 13.

Schuwer, L. "De zijnsleer van Martin Heidegger." Studia Catholica 26.

Wahl, J. L'idée d'être chez Heidegger. Paris.

1952 Benedikt, M. Das Problem des Grundes bei Martin Heidegger als ein Problem der Grundlegung oder Überwindung von Metaphysik. [Dissertation.] Wien.

Boss, M. "Die Bedeutung der Daseinsanalyse für die Psychologie und Psychiatrie." Psyche 6 (1952/53).

Wahl, J. Sur l'interpretation de l'histoire de la métaphysique d'après Heidegger. Paris.

1954 Wild, J. "The new empirism and human time." The Review of Metaphysics 7.

Berlinger, R. Das Nichts und der Tod. Frankfurt.

Hyppolite, J. Ontologie et phénoménologie chez Martin Heidegger." Les études philosophiques 9.

1955 Boer, W. de "Heideggers Mißverständnis der Metaphysik." *Zeitschrift für philosophische Forschung* 9.
1957 Schulz, W. *Der Gott in der neuzeitlichen Metaphysik*. Pfullingen.
1958 Dondeyne, A. "La différence ontologique chez Martin Heidegger." *Revue Philosophique de Louvain* 56.
     Uscatescu, G. "L'umanismo di Martin Heidegger." *Humanitas* 13.
1959 Ott, H. *Denken und Sein. Der Weg Martin Heideggers und der Weg der Theologie*. Zollikon.
     Pöggeler, O. "Sein als Ereignis." *Zeitschrift für philosophische Forschung* 13.
1960 Birault, H. "De l'Être, du Divin et des Dieux chez Heidegger." In *L'Existence de Dieu*. Tournai and Paris.
     ———"Heidegger et la pensée de la finitude." *Revue internationale de Philosophie* 14.
     Boehm, R. "Pensée et technique. Notes préliminaires pour une question touchant la problématique heideggerienne." *Revue internationale de Philosophie* 14.
     Grzesik, J. *Die Geschichtlichkeit als Wesensverfassung des Menschen. Eine Untersuchung zur Anthropologie W. Diltheys und M. Heideggers*. [Dissertation.] Bonn.
     Marx, W. "Heidegger und die Metaphysik." In *Beiträge zu Philosophie und Wissenschaft. Wilhelm Szilasi zum 70. Geburtstag*. München.
     Müller-Lauter, W. *Der Vorrang der Möglichkeit vor der Wirklichkeit im Denken Martin Heideggers*. [Dissertation.] Berlin.
     Noller, G. *Die Überwindung des Subjekt-Objekt-Schemas als philosophisches und theologisches Problem. Dargestellt an der Philosophie und an der Theologie der Entmythologisierung*. [Dissertation.] Tübingen.
1961 Gründer, K. "Martin Heideggers Wissenschaftskritik in ihren geschichtlichen Zusammenhängen." *Archiv für Philosophie* 11.
     Wiplinger, F. *Wahrheit und Geschichtlichkeit. Eine Untersuchung über die Frage nach dem Wesen der Wahrheit im Denken Martin Heideggers*. Freiburg and München.
1962 Wiele, J. van de. "*Res en Ding*. Bijdrage tot een vergelijkende studie van de zijnsopvatting in het thomisme en bij Heidegger." *Tijdschrift voor Philosophie* 24.
1963 Pöggeler, O. "Metaphysik und Seinstopik bei Heidegger." *Philosophisches Jahrbuch* 70 (1962/63).
     Demske, J. M. *Sein, Mensch und Tod. Das Todesproblem bei Martin Heidegger*. Symposion, vol. 12. Freiburg and München.

1964 Til, C. van. "The later Heidegger and theology." *Westminster Theological Journal* 26.

Wiele, J. van de. *Zijnswaarheid en onverborgenheid. Een vergelijkende studie over de ontologisch waarheid in het thomisme en bij Heidegger.* Leuven.

1965 Bretschneider, W. *Sein und Wahrheit. Uber die Zusammengehörigkeit von Sein und Wahrheit im Denken Martin Heideggers.* Monographien zur philosophischen Forschung, vol. 37. Meisenheim am Glan.

Pugliese, O. *Vermittlung und Kehre. Grundzüge des Geschichtsdenkens bei Martin Heidegger.* [Dissertation.] Symposion, vol. 18. Freiburg and München.

Versényi, L. *Heidegger, being and truth.* New Haven.

1966 Pflaumer, R. "Sein und Mensch im Denken Heideggers." *Philosophische Rundschau* 13.

Jong, A. de. *Een wijsbegeerte van het woord. Een godsdienstwijsgerige studie over de taalbeschouwing van Martin Heidegger.* Amsterdam.

1967 Manno, A. G. *Esistenza ed essere in Heidegger.* Pubblicazioni dell'Istituto di filosofia teoretica dell'Università di Napoli, vol. 7. Napoli.

1968 *Heidegger and the quest of truth.* Edited with an introduction by Manfred S. Frings. Chicago.

1970 Rosales, A. *Transzendenz und Differenz. Ein Beitrag zum Problem der ontologischen Differenz beim frühen Heidegger.* [Dissertation.] Phaenomenologica, vol. 33. The Hague.

1971 Couturier, F. *Monde et être chez Heidegger.* Preface by Bernard Welte. Montreal.

Maurer, R. "Von Heidegger zur praktischen Philosophie." In *Rehabilitierung der praktischen Philosophie.* Edited by M. Riedel. Freiburg.

1972 Herrmann, F. W. von. "Zeitlichkeit des Daseins und Zeit des Seins." *Perspektiven* 4.

AESTHETICS, POETRY, LANGUAGE

1952 Buddeberg, E. "Heidegger und die Dichtung." *Deutsche Vierteljahrsschrift f. Literaturwiss. u. Geistesgesch.* 26.

Fabro, C. "Ontologia dell'arte nell'ultimo Heidegger." *Giornale Critico della Filosofia Italiana,* Jg. 31, Ser. 3, Bd. 6.

Jaeger, H. "Heidegger's existential philosophy and modern German literature." *Publications of the Modern Language Association of America* 67.

1953 Buddeberg, E. "Heideggers Rilkedeutung." *Deutsche Vierteljahrsschrift f. Literaturwiss, und Geistesgesch.* 27.

Wahl, J. *La pensée de Heidegger et la poésie de Hölderlin.* Paris.

1954 Allemann, B. *Hölderlin und Heidegger.* Zürich and Freiburg. 2nd ed., 1956. Also contains "Heidegger und die Literaturwissenschaft."]

1955 Staiger, E. *Die Kunst der Interpretation. Studien zur deutschen Literaturgeschichte.* Zürich. Includes reprint of "Zu einem Vers von Mörike. Ein Briefwechsel mit Martin Heidegger," 1951.

1956 Buddeberg, E. *Denken und Dichten des Seins. Heidegger, Rilke.* Stuttgart.

1959 Jaeger, H. "Heidegger and the work of art." *Journal of Aesthetics and Art Criticism* 17 (1958/59).

1961 Schöfer, E. *Die Sprache Heideggers.* Pfullingen.

1964 Szondi, P. "Hölderlins Brief an Böhlendorff." *Euphorion* 58.

1965 Rifka, F. *Studien zur Ästhetik Heideggers und Oskar Beckers.* [Dissertation.] Tübingen.

1966 Bock, I. *Heideggers Sprachdenken.* [Dissertation.] Meisenheim am Glan.

1969 Biemel, W. "Dichtung und Sprache bei Heidegger." *Man and World* 2 and 4.

1971 Jaeger, H. *Heidegger und die Sprache.* Bern.

1972 Kockelmans, J. *On Heidegger and language.* Northwestern University Studies in Phenomenology and Existential Philosophy. Evanston, Ill. Includes:

I. Kockelmans, J., "Language, meaning, and ek-sistence"; and Aler, J., "Heidegger's conception of language in being and time";

II. Biemel, W., "Poetry and language in Heidegger."

Pöggeler, O., "Heidegger's topology of being";

Birault, H., "Thinking and poetizing in Heidegger";

Ott, H., "Hermeneutic and personal structure of language";

Kockelmans, J., "Ontological difference, hermeneutics, and language";

Marx, W., "The world in another beginning. Poetic dwelling and the role of the poet"; and

"Discussion."

III. Schöfer, E., "Heidegger's language. Metalogical forms of thought and grammatical specialities"; and
Lohmann, J. M., "Heidegger's 'Ontological Difference' and language."

INDIVIDUAL WORKS

1946 Koyré, A. "Vom Wesen der Wahrheit par Martin Heidegger (1943)." Fontaine 52.

1949 Brock, W. "An account of The four Essays. 1. A brief general characterisation of the four essays; 2. On the essence of truth; 3. The essay on F. Hölderlin; 4. What is metaphysics?" In Martin Heidegger. Existence and Being. London.

Krüger, G. "Martin Heidegger und der Humanismus. Zur Auseinandersetzung mit den Schriften Platons Lehre von der Wahrheit und Brief über den Humanismus." Studia philosophica 9. Reprinted in Theologische Rundschau 18 (1950).

1950 Aranguren, J. L. L. "Sobre Holzwege de Martin Heidegger." Arbor 16.

1951 Löwith, K. "Heideggers Kehre." Die neue Rundschau 62 and 64.

1952 Biemel, W., and A. de Waelhens. "Heideggers Schrift Vom Wesen der Wahrheit." Symposion 3.

1953 Löwith, K. "Heideggers Auslegung des Ungesagten in Nietzches Wort Gott ist tot." Die neue Rundschau 64.

Waelhens, A. de. Chemins et impasses de l'ontologie heideggerienne. A propos des Holzwege. Louvain and Paris.

Waelhens, A., W. Biemel. Introduction et commentaire zu: Martin Heidegger, Kant et le problème de la métaphysique. Paris.

1954 Bröcker, W. "Heidegger und die Logik. Zu Martin Heideggers Einführung in die Metaphysik. (Tübingen 1953)." Philosophische Rundschau 1 (1953/54).

Schulz, W. "Über den philosophie-geschichtlichen Ort Martin Heideggers. Philosophische Rundschau 1 (1953/54).

1955 Schilling, K. "Heideggers Interpretation der Philosophiegeschichte. Bemerkungen anläßlich des Erscheinens der Einführung in die Metaphysik. (1953)." Archiv für Rechts- und Sozialphilosophie 41.

1956 Wahl, J. Vers la fin de l'ontologie. Étude sur L'Introduction dans la métaphysique par Heidegger. Paris.

1959 Satô, Keiji. *Geijutsu no Honshitsu, Haideggâ no Geijutsu-Ron.* [The Nature of Art. Heidegger's Discussion of Art.] Tokyo.
1960 Gadamer, H. G. "Zur Einführung." In Martin Heidegger, *Der Ursprung des Kunstwerkes.* Stuttgart.
1961 Buchner, H. "Kotoba ni tsuite no Haideggâ no Ron-Kyn." [Heidegger's Discussion of Language.] *Kansaigakuin-Tetsugakukenkyû-nenpô, Nishinomiya* (November).

Feick, H. *Index zu Heideggers* Sein und Zeit. Tübingen.
1962 Chapelle, A. *L'Ontologie phénoménologique de Heidegger. Un commentaire de* Sein und Zeit. Coll. Enzyclopédie universitaire. Paris.

Ilting, K.-H. "Sein als Bewegtheit. Zu Heidegger. *Vom Wesen und Begriff der PHYSIS; Aristoteles Physik B 1." Philosophische Rundschau* 10.

Kaulbach, F. "Die kantische Lehre von Ding und Sein in der Interpretation Heideggers. (Zu: Heidegger, *Die Frage nach dem Ding* und *Kants These über das Sein.)" Kantstudien* 55.

Acknowledgments

3, from *Martin Heidegger. Zum 80. Gebertstag von seiner Heimatstadt Messkirch* (Vittorio Klostermann, Frankfurt, 1969); 7, 9, 12, 14, 19, 20, 21, 23, 27, 31, 43, 45, Ullstein-Bilderdienst, Berlin; 17, 28, 42, Staatsbibliothek Berlin; 18, 22, 47, Rowohlt Archiv; 29, from *Das archaische Griechenland* (Verlag C. H. Beck, München, 1969); 32, Jacques Robert, N.R.F.; 35, Foto Fritz Eschen, Berlin-Wilmersdorf; 44, Ringler Bilderdienst, A.G., Zurich; 46, Bilderdienst Süddeutscher Verlag; 52, Eric Schaal. All other photographs were supplied by Martin Heidegger.